MASTER LISTS FOR WRITERS

THE EXPANDED VOLUME OF
THE POPULAR WRITING
REFERENCE BOOK

GOLD EDITION

BRYN DONOVAN

ALSO BY BRYN DONOVAN

NONFICTION:

5,000 Writing Prompts
Blank Page to Final Draft
The Book of Dreams Come True

FICTION:

An Experienced Mistress
Sunrise Cabin (as Stacey Donovan)
Her Knight at the Museum
Her Time Traveling Duke

Print: 978-1-951952-14-3
Ebook: 978-1-951952-12-9

Cover design: Glendon Haddix at Streetlight Graphics

BrynDonovan.com

for G.

TABLE OF CONTENTS

INTRODUCTION

Welcome to the Gold Edition of *Master Lists for Writers*—the revised and expanded edition of the beloved book designed to help you stay inspired, write more, and reach your goals. My master lists have been used by writers and creators all over the world, and this book is a gold mine of inspiration for novels, scripts, memoirs, plays, short stories, essays, videogames, role-playing games, and more.

We writers have all had the experience of getting stuck in the middle of a scene and drawing a blank on something minor—from a facial expression, to a line of dialogue, to a detail in a particular setting. It can be so frustrating when such a simple thing grinds our writing to a halt! And when we're thinking about larger story issues, such as plot points, character motivations, and how characters grow and change over the course of the story, it can help to have a lot of idea starters at our fingertips.

That's why I began to create reference lists in notebooks for my own writing projects. I shared them on my blog, and some lists went viral. This inspired me to publish the first edition of *Master Lists for Writers*. Some people refer to my lists as "cheat sheets." But obviously, if you bought this book or checked it out of a library, it's not cheating! Other writers have told me that it's impossible to have writer's block when this book is close at hand.

Several times since publishing the first edition, I've had the surreal experience of meeting an author I admire…only to have them tell me, *Oh, I know who you are. I keep your book on my desk!* And it's just as much of an honor to be a part of the creative process of an unpublished author or an aspiring screenwriter.

This second edition is a much bigger book. Here's what I've done!

The first section of the book features lists of descriptions that many writers use over and over, which is why they're labeled "essential descriptions." I've expanded these lists, and I added a new one to describe voices.

I've added many new lists related to dialogue, character motivation, character development, plotting, action, setting, and more. I've also done some reorganizing. For the sake of space, I cut a few lists that fewer people needed, such as the lists of names from the U.S. Wild West in the 1800s and the names from Viking-era Scandinavia. I've put both of these lists on my blog, BrynDonovan.com, in case you still need them!

Many people have told me they wanted to give *Master Lists for Writers* as a gift to an aspiring author or a teen author, but they didn't because of a couple of adults-only lists in the first edition. To make the new edition more appropriate for giving, as well as more appropriate for libraries and high schools, I've eliminated the adults-only lists from this edition.

I know that not every list is useful to every writer. I've listened to lots of requests from my blog readers, my book editing clients, and other writers, and I've tried to make the volume as useful as possible.

There is no rhyme or reason to my use of pronouns in this book. I use "he," "she," and the singular "they," mostly at random. (*The Chicago Manual of Style,* the authoritative style guide for book publishing, accepts the use of the singular "they" in both informal and formal contexts.) I've also used the pronouns "one" and "you." It doesn't matter which pronouns I use, because I don't know the genders of your characters. In every case, substitute whatever pronouns you like.

It would be impossible to make any of these lists complete. What I love most about lists is that they often inspire additional ideas.

I don't use so-called AI tools such as ChatGPT for writing or for anything else. My writing process mostly consists of sitting on the couch and staring at the wall for such long periods of time that my dogs sometimes worry about me. Creating this book also entailed many long days and nights of research at my local library. At times, I would think that only a lunatic would put this much time into making lists. But from experience, I know I'll use them many times over the years and decades, and I'm sure you will, too.

If you enjoy *Master Lists for Writers: Gold Edition,* please consider leaving a review online: on Goodreads, Amazon, the Barnes & Noble website, Apple, Kobo, and/or Tertulia. You're allowed to leave a review on a site even if you didn't purchase the book there. This book is independently published, and I am a full-time author and freelance book editor. Your support means more than I can say.

If you think of a list you'd love to see, feel free to reach out to me through my blog and let me know. There's a possibility I'll create it for my blog.

Thank you again. I hope this book helps you as you do some of your most amazing creative work yet!

Happy writing!

Bryn Donovan

1. ESSENTIAL DESCRIPTIONS

Good description enables many readers to envision the characters, which makes the characters seem more real. And because so much of communication is nonverbal, if we write conversations without including short descriptions of facial expressions, body language, and gestures, we're leaving a lot out. It's easy to write more natural-sounding dialogue if the nonverbal cues are telling part of the story.

Facial expressions, body language, and gestures can also set up lines of dialogue without always having to write a "said" or "asked" tag. Although most readers sort of glide over "said" and "asked," once in a while, they can still become too repetitive on the page. Meanwhile, most successful authors prefer to use the synonyms to "said" and "asked" only sparingly, because they draw attention to themselves. Facial expressions, body language, and gestures can also make it easier to avoid using too many adverbs in dialogue. For instance, this:

"I won second place," Rachel said happily.

Might become this:

Rachel beamed. "I won second place."

Many of us find ourselves using the same handful of descriptions too often. This section provides alternatives.

For some readers, a little bit of physical description gives a character introduction more impact. It's easier for some people to keep a cast of characters straight in their heads if they have mental pictures of them. However, as writers, we don't have to write long passages describing our characters' looks. We might write that a black outfit makes a character look even more deathly pale than usual, or we might show a character pushing up their glasses or scratching their bald head as they talk.

If you struggle with describing characters and emotions, consider carrying a fiction journal with you—or just keep a journal on your phone. When you're bored in a meeting, a classroom, or a public place, you can try writing down descriptions of people. (Just don't let anyone catch you do it.) When you come across a descriptive passage you like in a novel, add it to your journal, too—not so you can steal it, obviously, but so that you can be inspired by it and try something similar in your writing. You can also read it aloud to get a better feel for how it's done.

DESCRIPTIONS OF FACIAL EXPRESSIONS

I've categorized these expressions under "positive and neutral," and "negative." I haven't organized them according to particular emotion, because so many of them work for more than one. A person might narrow his eyes out of vindictiveness or skepticism, for instance, and his face might turn red out of anger or embarrassment.

Some of these may require a little more explanation on your part. Depending on the context, you may need to tell the reader who they are glaring at, or whether their face is contorting in rage, or in grief. Keep in mind that not all of these will work for every character. It depends on what the character looks like and how they typically react to things.

A few things on this list aren't exactly facial expressions, but they're still useful for dialogue tags. I've often provided many ways to describe the same thing.

POSITIVE OR NEUTRAL EMOTIONS

she raised an eyebrow

he lifted an eyebrow

his right eyebrow shot up

he waggled his eyebrows

his eyes widened

her eyes bugged

his eyes lit up

her eyes darted

his gaze shifted

his gaze bounced back and forth

he squinted

she screwed up her eyes

she blinked

her eyes twinkled

his eyes gleamed

her eyes sparkled

his eyes flashed

her eyes glinted

her eyes were alive with excitement

his eyes shone with…

her eyes sparked with…

his eyes flickered with…

her eyes danced with…

affection glowed in his eyes

lust glittered in her eyes

the corners of her
eyes crinkled

his crow's feet deepened
as he smiled

she winked

his lashes fluttered

she batted her lashes

he feigned an
innocent look

she gaped in faux outrage

he gave a mock-stern look

his eyes widened in
pretend shock

she gave him a once-over

he sized her up

she took in the sight of…

his gaze raked over him

he eyed her

she gave him a
come-hither look

her gaze slid down
his body

she slipped him a
curious glance

her gaze met his

his gaze traveled to hers

he looked askance at her

she slid him a guarded look

he shot her a
surprised look

she peered

he gazed

she glanced

he stared

she scrutinized

he studied

she gaped

he looked thunderstruck

he observed

she surveyed

he swept the room
with a glance

she gave him a side eye

he gave her a
sidelong glance

she gawked

she ogled

he leered

he gave her a
puppy-dog look

his pupils (were) dilated

her pupils were huge

his pupils flared

he licked his lips

she moistened her lips

her lips parted

she smiled

he smirked

she grinned

he simpered

she beamed

he cracked a smile

a smile dawned on her face

a smile spread
across her face

a smile danced on his lips

her mouth curved
into a smile

her lips curved into
a brilliant smile

she gave them a
thousand-watt smile

he threw her a
dazzling smile

he gifted her with
a blinding smile

she treated him to
a rare smile

she gave her a broad smile

his smile revealed dimples

her smile showed a
dimple in her left cheek

the corners of his
mouth turned up

the corner of her
mouth quirked up

a smile tugged at his lips

a smile played at her lips

she said with an
impish smile

he said with a roguish smile

she gave them a
teasing smile

she gave him a
naughty smile

he gave a self-
deprecating smile

she attempted an
apologetic smile

she couldn't
suppress a smile

he flashed her a smile

a corner of her
mouth lifted

his mouth twitched

he gave a half-smile

she gave a lopsided grin

he pursed his lips

she stuck out her tongue

her mouth fell open

his jaw dropped

her jaw went slack

her whole face lit up

his expression lightened

she brightened

awe transformed his face

tenderness suffused
her features

relief washed over
his features

recognition dawned
on her face

his expression softened

NEGATIVE EMOTIONS

These include, but aren't limited to, sadness, anger, disgust, fear, anxiety, exhaustion, and embarrassment. Note that embarrassment can sometimes be positive, such as when a person gets a compliment that makes them blush.

his brows knitted

her forehead creased

his forehead furrowed

her forehead puckered

a line etched between
her brows

his brows drew together

her brows snapped
together

he raised his eyebrows

sweat beaded her forehead

perspiration shone
on his brow

her face glistened
with sweat

her eyes went round

terror flashed in his eyes

her eyelids drooped

his eyelids sagged

his eyes narrowed

she rolled her eyes

he looked heavenward

she glanced up
at the ceiling

he avoided her gaze

his eyes had a haunted look

tears filled her eyes

his eyes welled up

her eyes swam with tears

his eyes flooded with tears

her eyes were wet

his eyes glistened

tears shimmered
in her eyes

tears shone in his eyes

her eyes were glossy

he fought back tears

tears ran down her cheeks

his eyes closed

she squeezed her eyes shut

he shut his eyes

her eyes bored into him

his eyes burned with…

her eyes blazed with…

he pinned her with his gaze

she fixed him with
a gimlet stare

she gave him a frosty look

he cast her a veiled glance

her eyes shot sparks

he glared

her nose crinkled

his nose wrinkled

she sneered

his nostrils flared

she stuck her nose
in the air

he sniffed

she sniffled

his mouth twisted

her upper lip curled

he gave her a
mocking smile

she gave them a cruel smile

he grinned like a wolf

she smiled like an alligator

he plastered on a smile

she forced a smile

he faked a smile

her smile faded

his smile slipped

her smile wavered

his smile faltered

she switched off her smile

she pouted

his mouth snapped shut

her mouth set in a hard line

he pressed his lips together

her lips were compressed

she bit her lip

he worried his bottom lip

she nibbled on
her bottom lip

he chewed on his
bottom lip

his jaw set

her jaw clenched

his jaw tightened

a muscle in her
jaw twitched

a muscle in his jaw jumped

a muscle in her jaw flexed

she was grinding her teeth

he gritted his teeth

he ground his jaw

he snarled

her lips drew back
in a snarl

she gnashed her teeth

her lower lip trembled

his lower lip quivered

she paled

he blanched

she went white

the color drained
from his face

his face reddened

her cheeks turned pink

his face flushed

she blushed

he turned red

she turned scarlet

he turned crimson

a flush crept up her face

heat stained her cheeks

he screwed up his face

she scrunched up her face

he had a hangdog
expression

he grimaced

she winced

she gave him a dirty look

he frowned

she scowled

he glowered

his face went blank

she went poker-faced

his face was motionless

she affected a bland
expression

her face took on a
stoic expression

his expression was
unreadable

she wore an unfathomable
expression

her face was a mask

he assumed a wooden
expression

her expression hardened

a grim expression
cemented his features

her face contorted

his face twisted

her expression closed up

his expression dulled

his expression sobered

a vein popped out
on his neck

fear crossed her face

sadness clouded
his features

DESCRIPTIONS OF GESTURES AND BODY LANGUAGE

Many of these can evoke different emotions in different contexts. Your protagonist, for instance, might lift her chin in confidence, or in angry defiance. Your villain might rub his hands together because he's planning evil things, or because it's cold in his lair. Because of this wide disparity of uses, I haven't attempted to separate these into positive and negative emotions.

Some items on this list may not be gestures or body language, exactly, but may be useful for setting up dialogue. As with the list of facial expressions, I've included some different ways to say the same thing.

Each of your characters may have one or two gestures that are typical of them. While you wouldn't want to overdo it, this can make the people in your story feel more real.

she nodded

he bobbed his head

she tilted her head

he cocked his head

she inclined her head

he jerked his head toward…

she threw her head back

he lowered his head

she hung her head

he ducked

he looked away

she averted her gaze

he stared at the floor

she dropped her gaze

she bowed her head

he put his head in his hands

he covered his eyes with a hand

she hid behind her book

she pressed her hands to her cheeks

he clapped his hands to his face

she raised her chin

he lifted his chin

her hands squeezed
into fists

his hands tightened
into fists

she clenched her fists

she balled her fists

he unclenched his fists

her arms remained
at her sides

his arms dangled
at his sides

he shrugged

she gave a half shrug

he lifted his shoulder
in a half shrug

he gave a Gallic shrug

she gave a dismissive
wave of her hand

she raised a hand
in greeting

he waved

he held up a hand
to silence her

he lifted his hands

she held up her palms

he threw his hands
in the air

she brushed her
palms together

he rubbed his
hands together

she made a steeple
of her fingers

he placed his
fingertips together

he spread his hands

she gesticulated

she fanned herself

he flapped his hands

he waved his hands

she clapped her hands

he snapped his fingers

she held up a finger

she wagged a finger

he pointed

she gestured with a thumb

he jerked his thumb
toward…

he cupped his
hand to his ear

she extended her middle
finger toward him

he gave her the finger

she flipped him the bird

she gave him the
thumbs up

he gave him the okay sign

she flashed a peace sign

she drew a finger
across her throat

he twirled a finger
next to his temple

he crossed himself

she pressed her
hands together in the
"namaste" gesture

she saluted

he touched two fingers
to his forehead in
a mock salute

he flexed his hands
near his head, as if to
say "mind blown"

she made a V-sign and
pointed two fingers at
her eyes, then at him

he brought his fingers
to his lips in a "chef's
kiss" gesture

she pursed his lips and
made a kissing sound

he pretended to
flex his muscles

she struck a cute pose with
her hand under her chin

she made a heart shape
with her hands

he held up his palms
and did jazz hands

he twirled his finger,
indicating that she
should do a spin

he pretended to shoot
himself in the head

she shot finger
guns at them

he clamped his hands
over his ears

she pressed her
fingers to her ears

he pressed one finger
to his ear as he talked
on the phone

she waggled her hips

he thrust his pelvis

he put his hands
on his hips

she rested a hand
on her hip

she jutted out her hip

she shoved her hands
into her pockets

he jammed his hands
in his pockets

she folded her arms

he crossed his arms
over his chest

she hugged herself

he wrapped his arms
around himself

she rubbed her forearms

she spread her arms wide

he held out his arms

she held out her hand
(for money or an object)

he reached out his hands
in a grabby motion

he extended a hand

he shook his head

she turned her face away

he looked away

his breaths quickened

she panted

she was breathing hard

his chest rose and fell
with rapid breaths

she took in a deep breath

he drew in a long breath

she took in a sharp breath

he gasped

she sucked in a breath

she held her breath

he let out a harsh breath

she exhaled

he blew out his cheeks

she blew out a breath

she huffed

he sighed

she snorted

she laughed

he giggled

she guffawed

he chuckled

she gave a bitter laugh

he gave a mirthless laugh

he gave a rueful chuckle

she tittered

he cackled

she rubbed her shoulder

he kneaded his shoulder

he rolled his shoulders

she tensed her shoulders

he massaged the
back of his neck

she rubbed her temples

she rubbed her hands
on her thighs

she ran her hand
through her hair

he threaded a hand
through his hair

he raked his fingers
through his hair

he shoved his hair
away from his face

she toyed with a
lock of hair

she played with her hair

she twirled her hair

she wrapped a curl
around her finger

she tucked a lock of
hair behind her ear

he undid his ponytail

she shook out her hair

he tossed his hair

he buried his hands
in his hair

he tugged at his hair

he stroked his beard/chin

he scratched his beard

she tugged at her earlobe

they bit a nail

she chewed on a cuticle

she picked at her nails

she inspected her
fingernails

he touched his scar

he picked at the scab

he plucked at the
cuff of his shirt

she picked lint
from her sleeve

he adjusted the lapels
of his jacket

he glanced at his watch

she tapped her watch

she adjusted her bra

she fiddled with her earring

he twisted the ring
on his finger

he tugged at his shirt collar

he adjusted his tie

she smoothed
down her skirt

she scratched her nose

he scratched his head

she rubbed her forehead

she slapped her forehead

he smacked his forehead

he facepalmed

she rubbed her eyes

she pinched the
bridge of her nose

he held his nose

he slapped a hand
over his mouth

she covered her mouth
with her hand

he slapped his knee

she pressed her
fingers to her lips

he tapped his fingers
against his lips

she held her finger
up to her lips

he rubbed his chin

she pressed a hand
to her throat

she touched her
hand to her heart

he pounded his chest

he clutched his chest

he leaned against the wall

she bounced on her toes

he danced in place

she jumped up and down

he tapped his foot

he stomped his foot

her toes curled

she folded her
hands in her lap

she drummed her
fingers on the table

he tapped his fingers
on the table

he slammed his hand
on the counter

she pounded her fist
on the counter

she set her palms down
flat on the desk

he rested his hands
on the desk

she set her hands on
the table, palms up

he leaned back in his chair

she hooked her feet
around the chair legs

he gripped the arm
of the chair

she put her hands
behind her head

he put his feet up
on the desk

he fidgeted

she jiggled her foot

he swung his leg

she crossed her legs

he uncrossed his legs

she crossed her ankles
in front of her

she stretched out her
legs in front of her

he sprawled out

she cringed

he shuddered

she flinched

he recoiled

he shivered

she trembled

his body shook

she cowered

he shrank back

she huddled in the corner

he pulled away

she jerked away

he turned away

she stilled

he froze

she jolted upright

he stiffened

she straightened

they tensed

he jumped

she jumped to her feet

he stood up

she rose from her seat

she relaxed

he hunched

she slouched

her shoulders sagged

his shoulders slumped

her shoulders rounded

he rolled his shoulders

his chest caved

he drooped

she wilted

he went limp

she squared her shoulders

he clasped his hands
behind his back

she clasped her hands
in front of her

he puffed out his chest

she thrust out her chest

he propped his chin
on his hand

she rested her chin
on her palm

he yawned

she stretched

he turned around

she whirled around

she spun around

he pivoted

she reeled

he staggered

her knees buckled

she stepped away

she drew nearer

he leaned closer

she inched forward

he loomed closer

he paced

she shifted from one
foot to the other

she rocked back and forth

he shuffled his feet

he swayed on his feet

she dragged her feet

he pumped a fist

she shook imaginary
pompons

he thrust his fists in the air

she punched the air

PHYSICAL DESCRIPTIONS
OF CHARACTERS

Many readers have an easier time of keeping different characters straight in their heads when they know what the characters look like. Physical description can also make characters feel more real.

Some writers may be tempted to use physical traits as shorthand for personality traits: the buxom blonde who's vapid, the heavyset man who's lazy. These stereotypes run the risk of reducing characters to caricatures, making the story feel less real and complex.

When you're in a character's point of view, their attitude toward someone else's appearance may change over the course of the story. A classic case in point: Mr. Darcy goes from saying Elizabeth Bennet is "tolerable, but not handsome enough to tempt me," to one of the handsomest women of his acquaintance, revealing that he's falling in love with her.

Some of these phrases on this list may be a little expected, but then again, characters may use familiar phrases in dialogue. Besides, you can always put your own spin on them!

EYES—GENERAL

big	watchful	shifty
large	alert	soulless
sloe ("sloe-eyed")	keen	soulful
small	penetrating	drooping
narrow	piercing	soft
sharp	intense	gentle
shrewd	squinty	honest
wary	like slits	childlike

doll-like

guileless

dreamy

glazed

unfocused

glassy

blank

vacant

expressionless

wild

round

lopsided

wide-set

close-set

deep-set

like deep pools

sunken

hollow

bulging

protruding

wide

hooded

heavy-lidded

bedroom

smoldering

stormy

beautiful

lovely

bright

bright as coins

brilliant

shining

liquid

crystalline

lustrous

lively

merry (antiquated)

dancing

flashing

glistening

glowing

sparkling

glittering

twinkling

smiling

laughing

mocking

dull

rheumy

bleary

watery

misty

milky

cloudy

bloodshot

red-rimmed

swollen

puffy

beady

birdlike

cat-like

puppy-like (or just "puppy eyes")

doe-like (or just "doe eyes")

jewel-like

unblinking

steely

flinty

hard

cold

dead

with thick eyelashes

fringed with long lashes

with sweeping eyelashes

heavy-lashed

with sparse lashes

dark circles beneath

dark circles
like bruises

traces of darkness
beneath

purple half
circles beneath

violet half
moons beneath

faint shadows
underneath

deep smudges
beneath

bags underneath

heavy bags
beneath

EYES – COLOR

Brown is the most common eye color by far, followed by blue and hazel. Truly black irises and purple irises are both extremely rare in real life, but somewhat more common in fantasy fiction.

ink-black

like wells of ink

obsidian

onyx

like black holes

coal black

raven black

midnight

jet black

chestnut

warm brown

russet brown

chocolate brown

like melted
chocolate

cocoa brown

coffee brown

espresso

mocha

mahogany

sepia

sienna

mink brown

the brown of
chestnuts

the brown of
polished wood

copper

amber

butterscotch

caramel

cognac

whiskey

brandy

sherry

the color of
mulled cider

honey

tawny

topaz

hazel

ringed with gold

with gold flecks

amethyst

violet

the purple
of twilight

sky-blue

sunny blue

cornflower blue

steel blue

ice blue

cold blue

chilly blue

Arctic blue

glacial blue

cerulean

sapphire

cobalt

electric blue

blue as
forget-me-nots

blue as propane
flame

azure

lake blue

ocean blue

Caribbean blue

Mediterranean
blue

aquamarine

turquoise

denim blue

storm blue

silver

chrome

platinum

pewter

charcoal

pebble gray

stone gray

smoky gray

ash gray

slate gray

cloud gray

gray as the
winter sky

dove gray

wolf gray

concrete gray

shark gray

fog gray

gunmetal gray

the color of
cement

gray as his hair

olive

emerald

jade

sage

fern green

leaf green

forest green

moss green

the green of
summer grass

green as the hills

EYEBROWS

straight	sparse	well-defined
arched	barely-there	perfectly shaped
rounded	light	severe
slanted	faint	full
angular	delicate	dark
high	thin	lush
penciled	skinny	bold
drawn on	fine	thick
plucked	scraggly	heavy
tweezed	unkempt	bushy
microbladed	elegant	craggy

grizzled	beetle-browed	unibrow
unruly	meeting in	
wild	the middle	

EYEGLASSES

While glasses aren't part of the body, I decided to add this section because they are often a part of a person's consistent look.

bespectacled	nerd-chic glasses
round glasses	smudged glasses
square glasses	glasses with thick lenses
rectangular glasses	glasses too big for her face
tortoiseshell glasses	glasses too small for his face
horn-rimmed glasses	eyes magnified behind his glasses
steel-rimmed glasses	
wire-framed glasses	light glinting off her eyeglasses
rimless glasses	
cat-eye glasses	glasses askew
aviator-style glasses	glasses slipping down on his nose
glasses with oversized rims	
glasses with thick frames	glasses perched on the end of her nose

SKIN – TEXTURE

Some of these are better for describing the face, and some are better for other parts of the body.

lined	seamed	withered
wrinkled	leathery	crepey
creased	weathered	thin

delicate

like parchment

sagging

drooping

loose

slack

taut

firm

clear

smooth

smooth as marble

silky/silken

satiny

translucent

like glass

radiant

luminous

glowing

moisturized

dewy

oily

waxy

fresh

baby-soft

youthful

flawless

poreless

flaky

scaly

dry

dehydrated

ashy

with large pores

dull

velvety

fuzzy

downy

hairy

rough

coarse

uneven

dimpled

orange-peel

doughy

blotchy

chapped

pimply

broken out

with rosacea

with broken capillaries

cheeks crisscrossed with broken veins

nose interlaced with broken veins

pockmarked

blemished

pitted

scarred

ravaged

puckered

bruised

veined

scratched

raw

SKIN – COLOR

Descriptions of the skin tone can be, unsurprisingly, a sensitive issue. Many readers object to writers, particularly white writers, comparing deeper skin tones to food—especially the more frequently used coffee, chocolate, and mocha. Please note that some of these descriptors don't refer to the skin's natural tone ("jaundiced," for instance.)

amber

bronze

beige

fawn

topaz

cinnamon

copper

brown

dark brown

deep brown

coffee

chocolate

mocha

ebony

mahogany

honey

caramel

dulce de leche

golden

ocher

sallow

pale

pallid

chalky

ghostly

pasty

wan

colorless

fair

light

creamy

alabaster

ivory

bisque

pearly

porcelain

white

milk-white

snow-white

white as paper

white as mayonnaise

lily-white

vanilla

warm

cool

olive

peach/peaches and cream

pink

rosy

blooming

ruddy

florid

russet

terra cotta

tawny

café au lait

like gingerbread

like strong tea

like tea with milk

like whiskey

mottled

liver-spotted

age-dappled

freckled

suntanned

sunburned

red as a lobster

sun-kissed

jaundiced

gray with exhaustion/pain

gray as the dawn

FACE—STRUCTURE

square

round

oblong

oval

elongated

symmetrical

asymmetrical

narrow

gaunt

cadaverous

broad

full

plump

soft

apple-cheeked

baby-faced

chubby cheeks

cherubic

heart-shaped

moon-faced

catlike

leonine

foxlike

wolfish

rat-like

like a bulldog

with heavy jowls

elfin

delicate

fine bone structure

sloped forehead

high forehead

broad forehead

prominent brow ridge

protruding brow bone

sharp cheekbones

cheekbones sharp as blades

cheekbones sharp as knives

high cheekbones

angular cheekbones

wide cheekbones

hollow cheeks

sunken cheeks

square jaw

lantern-jawed

chiseled

sculpted

hard-featured

craggy

jutting chin

pointed chin

weak chin

receding chin

double chin

cleft chin

dimple in chin

large Adam's apple

protruding Adam's apple

NOSE

small

dainty

button

upturned

perky

long

large

prominent

broad

thick

thin

straight

pointed

sharp

flat

crooked

hooked

aquiline

aristocratic

Nubian

Roman

Grecian

bulbous

bony

fleshy

flared

strong

hawk

rat-like

MOUTH/LIPS

thin

narrow

small

large

wide

full

generous

lush

luscious

thick

plump

enhanced
with filler

bee-stung

Cupid's bow

pouting

rosebud

soft

hard

firm

dry

cracked

chapped

moist

wet

glossy

lacquered

painted

even teeth

straight teeth

crooked teeth

gap between teeth

gleaming
white teeth

yellowed teeth

overbite

underbite

FACIAL HAIR (OR LACK THEREOF)

clean-shaven

smooth-shaven

stubble

scruff

a few days'
growth of beard

five o'clock
shadow

neatly trimmed
beard

short/long beard

full beard

bushy beard

patchy beard

scruffy beard

neckbeard

goatee

soul patch

Van Dyke beard

chinstrap beard

lumberjack beard

biker beard

Amish beard

forked beard

a faint mustache

an attempt at
a mustache

1970s mustache

handlebar
moustache

pencil moustache

walrus moustache

sideburns

mutton chops

HAIR

long	scraggly	full
short	straggly	wild
shoulder-length	bushy	bouncy
loose	frizzy	coarse
limp	wavy	fine
listless	beachy waves	neatly combed
flat	curly	parted
dull	straight	slicked down
shiny	stringy	slicked back
glossy	lanky	shaved
sleek	dirty	comb-over
smooth	oily	cropped
luminous	greasy	clipped
lustrous	dry	buzzed
spiky	split ends	buzz cut
stringy	fried	crewcut
shaggy	thin/thinning	fade
tousled	bald	undercut
windblown	thick	pixie cut
tangled	luxuriant	bob
messy	flowing	layers
untamed	corkscrews	afro
unmanageable	coils	puffs
matted	spirals	braids
a rat's nest	ringlets	twists
unkempt	widow's peak	dreadlocks
bedhead	voluminous	locs

Bantu knots

box braids

cornrows

French braid

crown braid

fishtail braid

plaits

pigtails

ponytail

chignon

bun/messy bun

updo

pompadour

bouffant

beehive

mullet

perm

blunt bangs

feathered
(of bangs)

fringe

baby bangs

side-swept bangs

Birkin bangs

French-girl bangs

extensions

wig-like

looked like a wig

HAIR—COLOR

black

blue-black

jet black

coal black

obsidian

onyx

raven

ebony

black as basalt

ink black

midnight black

salt and pepper

threaded
with silver

silver

charcoal gray

steel gray

smoke gray

white

snow white/
snowy

brunette

sable

mink brown

chocolate brown

mahogany

coffee brown

the color of
brown sugar

mousy brown

nut brown

hazelnut

caramel

praline brown

toffee brown

chestnut

cinnamon

the color of
old pennies

red

cherry cola red

burgundy

auburn

Titian-haired

russet

copper

ginger

fiery red

the color of flame

strawberry blonde

butterscotch

honey

wheat

amber

blonde

golden

sandy blond

brassy blond

dirty blond

dishwater blond

ash blond

platinum blond

champagne blond

flaxen

the color of
corn silk

fair-haired

tinted

dyed

an unnatural
black/blonde/red

implausibly
black/blonde/red

bleached

sun-streaked

ombré

dark roots

gray roots

grown out to
reveal silver roots

highlights

balayage

HANDS

small

soft

soft as a child's

delicate

slender

elegant

spidery

square

large

strong

meaty

paw-like

dry

moist

sweaty

dirty

stained

rough

calloused

with prominent
veins

blue-veined

stubby fingers

long fingers

crooked fingers

gnarled fingers

manicured

neat fingernails

clean fingernails

with long nails

with ragged
cuticles

ragged fingernails

bitten-down
fingernails

dirty fingernails

grimy fingernails

BODY

short

petite

tiny

compact

average height

tall

towering

big

large

heavy

heavy-set

fat

overweight

obese

corpulent

flabby

burly

beefy

bulky

bear-like

like a teddy
bear

hearty

stocky

hefty

pudgy

pot-bellied

paunchy

portly

thick

stout

robust

chunky

chubby

plump

lush

plush

soft

Rubenesque

zaftig

full-figured

plus-sized

ample

rounded

generous

ripe

voluptuous

nubile

buxom

curvy/
curvaceous

hourglass

wasp-waisted

pear-shaped

nymph-like

sylph-like

sprite-like

leggy

long-legged

coltish

gangling

lanky

rangy

raw-boned

fine-boned

lissome

willowy

lithe

lean

lean as a whip

svelte

slim

slender

slight

trim

spare

wiry

thin

skinny

emaciated

bony

frail

skeletal

gaunt

with a baby bump

very pregnant

heavily pregnant

ropy

sinewy

sturdy

fit

toned

athletic

muscular

well-built

strapping

powerful

Herculean

hulking

brawny

ripped

chiseled

sloping shoulders

broad-shouldered

barrel-chested

flat-chested

sunken-chested

bullnecked

DESCRIPTIONS OF VOICES

These are adjectives, but some of them can be altered into verbs ("braying"/"brayed") or nouns ("raspy"/"his voice was a rasp.") Some of these describe a voice quality, and some of them describe tone. A few of these also suggest habitual speech patterns.

You may not need to describe an emotional tone of voice much of the time. Facial expressions, body language, or the dialogue itself may make it clear. However, sometimes you might, particularly when the tone of voice does not match what the person is saying.

abrasive	bland	childish
acidic	bleak	chirping
adenoidal	blunt	choked
airy	booming	clear
animated	brash	clipped
anxious	braying	cloying
authoritative	breathy	coarse
barbed	breezy	cold
barely audible	bright	cool
baritone	brisk	complacent
barking	brittle	contented
bass	broken	contralto
big	bubbly	cracked/ cracking
blasé	burbling	
bombastic	calm	creaky
bored	caustic	croaking
boyish	casual	crisp
bitter	cheery/ cheerful	crooning
		curt

cultured

cynical

deep

devoid of emotion

discordant

dispirited

drawling

dreamy

dry

dulcet

dull

earnest

easy

falsetto

faint

feathery

feeble

firm

flat

fierce

forceful

fretful

gentle

ghostly

girlish

glum

goofy

grating

grave

gravelly/ like gravel

grim

groggy

growling

gruff

guttural

hard

harsh

hateful

haunted

hearty

hesitant

high/ high-pitched

hissing

hoarse

honeyed

hushed

husky

immense

indifferent

insinuating

intense

ironic

jubilant

lazy

lifeless

light

lilting

lively

loud

loving

low/ low-pitched

matter-of-fact

mellifluous

melodic

mild

mocking

monotonous

muffled

musical

muted

nasal

nasty

neutral

nonchalant

obsequious

oily

piercing

piping

plaintive

polished

quavering

querulous

quiet

ragged

raspy	sleepy	squeaky
raucous	sluggish	squealing
raw	slurred	sweet
reedy	sly	sympathetic
refined	small	tart
resonant	smarmy	teasing
ringing	smoky	thick
roaring	smooth	thin
robust	snide	throaty
rough	soft	thunderous
rumbling	solid	tight
saccharine	somber	tender
sarcastic	sonorous	tense
savage	soothing	trembling
scornful	soprano	tremulous
scratchy	sour	trilling
screeching	spacey/	uncertain
serene	spaced-out	unctuous
severe	stark	unsteady
shaky	steely	vague
sharp	stiff	velvet/velvety
shrill	stout	warm
sibilant	strained	wavering
silken/like silk	strident	weak
silly	stony	weary
silvery	suave	wheezy
sincere	sugary	whiny
singsong	suggestive	wistful
sleek	surly	

DESCRIPTIONS OF HOW EMOTIONS FEEL

As writers, we convey many feelings through actions, dialogue, facial expressions, body language, and gestures. However, we sometimes need good ways to describe the way emotions feel. If we only write things like, "He felt sad," "she felt angry," "he was devastated," or "she was elated," the reader won't feel much at all.

This list focuses on two other ways we can make emotions more vivid: by assigning an active verb to them, and by describing how the emotions feel in the body. Physiological reactions to emotions should be used judiciously, but when you're writing about a strong feeling, they're a good way to elicit a reader response.

Please note that you can turn almost any of these into a supporting phrase in your story. For instance, *humiliation overcame her* can become *overcome with humiliation*. You can use a physiological response, such as tensed muscles or an increased heart rate, without naming an emotion that is obvious in context.

I've focused on some basic, primal emotions: anger, fear, disgust, shame, sadness, and joy. You may find inspiration here for describing other feelings as well.

ANGER

her annoyance flared

he quivered with indignation

his every muscle tensed

her body was taut with anger

every muscle knotted with rage

her body locked up with rage

she could barely keep her anger in check

he struggled to
contain his temper

his teeth clenched

her anger pulsed
like a current

she simmered with anger

he trembled with fury

his blood boiled

anger seared through her

her pulse slammed
in her neck

he shook with fury

anger roared through him

rage swept over him

anger rolled through her

her temples throbbed
with rage

his brain exploded
with fury

fury blinded her

rage poisoned her veins

anger swelled up in him

rage fueled her

flames of anger
shot through her

fury poured through her

she choked on her anger

anger crashed through him

rage flashed through her

FEAR

his breath shook

her hands trembled

she was barely able
to breathe

an alarm rang in her mind

she bit back a scream

his heart pounded

her heart drummed

his heart hammered
in his chest

his heart thudded

her chest stuttered

his heart was in his throat

fear splintered his heart

his chest tightened
with fear

worry snaked through her

worry gnawed at her

anxiety swirled around her

fear clawed through her

he shivered

fear twisted her gut

she felt dread in the
pit of her stomach

he felt a sinking feeling
in his stomach

his stomach knotted

sweat trickled
down his spine

her blood ran cold

a chill went through him

it chilled his soul

fear hit her like icy water

fear paralyzed her

panic assailed him

her mouth turned dry

gooseflesh crept
up her arms

DISGUST

she drew back

she battled the
urge to recoil

she forced down
a sick feeling

he suppressed a shudder

she fought the urge
to throw up

a wave of nausea hit him

she wanted to puke

he tasted bile

bitterness filled her mouth

she gagged

it sickened him

he cringed with disgust

his gorge rose

it turned her stomach

nausea rolled
through his belly

her stomach roiled

his stomach revolted

her stomach heaved

his stomach churned

it made her skin crawl

she wanted to purge the
images from her brain

SHAME

embarrassment
stirred in her

shame spiraled
through him

embarrassment seized her

he burned with humiliation

his scalp prickled
with shame

heat crept into her cheeks

she cringed inwardly

embarrassment racked her

guilt tormented him

guilt consumed her
from within

she floundered in
embarrassment

shame corroded his insides

shame washed over him

humiliation overcame her

guilt flooded over her

shame engulfed him

he wanted to disappear

she wanted to curl
up in shame

she wanted to die
on the spot

inwardly, he winced

he wanted the earth
to swallow him up

embarrassment
coiled around him

she wanted to slink away

SADNESS

sorrow closed up
her throat

his hopes disintegrated

he descended into
depression

his throat clenched

her throat thickened
with sobs

disappointment sagged
through him

his vision blurred

it plunged him into despair

his throat tightened

she was drowning
in her grief

pain gripped her chest

sadness tore at his chest

sorrow shredded
her insides

her heart wrenched

it stabbed his heart

his body felt leaden

a weight settled
on her heart

despair dragged her down

dejection burdened her

he crumbled inside

grief hollowed her out

his mood plummeted

grief shattered him

he felt an elevator-drop
in his stomach

he felt empty inside

she felt cold

her spirits fell

sadness crushed him

his bones ached
he could hardly move

numbness infused
her body
she felt numb all over

JOY

elation bubbled up in her

he glowed inside

joy overwhelmed her

it lifted her mood

it buoyed her spirits

her hopes rose

happiness flowed
through her

warmth filled his chest

joy filled him like sunshine

happiness sparkled
inside her

happiness warmed
him from within

her heart felt light

his heart leaped

she got a warm,
fuzzy feeling

joy welled up in her heart

hope fluttered inside her

joy danced through
her heart

her hopes kindled

happiness bloomed
inside her

joy blossomed within her

fresh energy filled him

exultation surged
through him

happiness coursed
through her

excitement raced
through her

they felt a jolt of
excitement

elation suffused his being

she felt fully alive

his spirits soared

she felt weightless

he felt light on his feet

she felt like she
was floating

he felt giddy

it felt like a caffeine buzz

she felt drunk with
happiness

DESCRIPTIONS OF PAIN

Some of these could also be adapted to writing about emotional pain.

she braced herself
for the pain

a dull ache

a bone-deep ache

a throbbing ache

his head throbbed

pain filled her head

pain squeezed her head

her eyes stung
with tiredness

his eyes felt like they
were burning

his eyes felt raw

her eyes felt gritty

she felt like she had
sand in her eyes

gnawing hunger

feeling hollow with hunger

hunger clawed at
her insides

his insides twisted
with hunger

a jab of pain

a burst of pain

a flash of pain

prickles of pain

a blaze of pain

fresh pain

a stinging pain

a spike of pain

white-hot pain

a sharp pain

a shooting pain

a stabbing pain

a piercing pain

a corrosive pain

a crippling pain

a searing pain

a grating pain

a grinding pain

a drumbeat of pain

pain shot up her leg

pain surged through
her body

pain lashed across
his lower back

Bryn Donovan

pain ripped through
her chest

pain branched across
their back like lightning

pain lacerated her shoulder

pain twisted his belly

a cramp seized her foot

pain exploded behind
her eyeballs

the pain flared in his leg

a flaming pain in her wrist

a burning pain in her neck

pain coursed
through his body

pain like a sharp
knife in his gut

pain went through her
like a sword/spear

pain lanced through him

blinded with pain

dizzy from the pain

disoriented from the pain

the pain blossomed
in his midsection

the pain spread
through her bowels

a wave of pain rolled
through her

pain crashed through
his body

he let out a gasp
from the pain

she panted with pain

she hissed

he grimaced

he managed to grin
through the pain

he winced at the pain

she cringed at the pain

they strained
against the pain

she curled up in pain

he doubled over
with agony

she writhed

he moaned

she sucked in a
sharp breath

he howled

she grunted from the pain

a cry of pain escaped him

she bit back a cry of pain

she yelped

he let out a shriek of pain

he screeched in pain

she screamed in pain

the pain brought
tears to his eyes

he quivered with pain

he was wracked by pain

she trembled from the pain

she was shaking
from the torment

she convulsed with pain

his breathing was shallow

the pain took her
breath away

he tried to breathe
through it

she tried to focus
on something other
than the pain

he clutched his
head in agony

she clamped her hand
around her stubbed toe

he cradled his
wounded arm

he grasped her hand
tightly as the pain hit

he clenched his teeth
when the pain hit

she gritted her teeth
against the pain

his face was drawn
with pain

her face was twisted
in anguish

she stiffened

he went rigid with agony

her back arched
off the bed

she spoke haltingly
from the pain

his voice was tight
with pain

her voice was
rough with pain

it hurt too much
for him to speak

pain like he'd never
felt before

agony robbed her of
rational thought

he was out of his
mind with pain

she was delirious with pain

he prayed for an end
to the suffering

she wished for the
release of death

he blacked out
from the pain

the pain abated

the pain eased

the drugs softened the pain

the pain faded

the pain diminished

the pain evaporated

the pain dissolved

the pain released her

the agony subsided

the pain dulled

the pain drained
out of her body

MAKING METAPHORS

A metaphor or simile is a comparison of one thing to another. It can often make a reader think about something in a new way. It might even stick with the reader for a long time.

In order to work, a metaphor needs to line up with the point of view and the tone of the story. A funny character's wit might be expressed through the hilarious comparisons she makes in her mind, while poetic metaphors might add to a soulful narrative. The immersive world of a fantasy or science fiction novel may be underscored by the use of metaphor.

For some writers, metaphorical language comes naturally. For others, it can be learned like anything else. I want to share one method that can help you write them, which I first used when I was teaching a beginning poetry writing workshop at university.

Divide a piece of paper into three columns. In the first column, write down a few concrete nouns—that is, nouns you can see, hear, or feel. For example, you might write down *blue jay* or *geode*.

In the middle column, write down a few adjectives that describe each noun. For *blue jay*, you might write down *vivid* or *argumentative*. It's okay if you use some phrases instead of words. For *geode*, you might put down *sparkly on the inside*.

In the third column, without thinking about it too much, write down other nouns that these adjectives or phrases could describe. *Argumentative* could also describe cranky children. *Sparkly on the inside* could describe a brain full of daydreams.

Now, you should see some beginnings of metaphors. For instance, you could write, "Outside my window, blue jays argued like cranky children," or, "The geode sparkled inside, like a brain full of daydreams."

Some of these will work better than others, and some won't work at all, but it's a good way to get to new ideas. If you read a lot of poetry and novels that use metaphorical language, and if you practice coming up with comparisons, metaphors are more likely to pop into your head as you write.

2. PLOTTING AND MOTIVATION

This section includes many ideas about conflict, which is at the heart of most stories. Without enough conflict, a story can be boring or unrealistic. Even the first list of character goals can inspire conflict in a story: obstacles can get in the way of what your protagonist wants.

For a plot to be truly engaging, we need to understand the characters' motivations for doing what they do. The more dramatic a decision or action is, the more important it is that we understand the reason behind it.

Some of the plot ideas in this section are more specific than others. However, each one can be handled in countless different ways. They're just idea starters, and it's the way you develop them that will make them great.

50 CHARACTER GOALS

1. Get a new job.

2. Graduate, or get accepted into a college.

3. Assassinate a monarch or overthrow a tyrant.

4. Make a fortune—or get out of debt.

5. Move to the city of their dreams.

6. Visit a faraway country or planet.

7. Learn a foreign language.

8. Adopt a pet.

9. Lose weight.

10. Get elected to public office.

11. Figure out who the killer is.

12. Rob a bank, palace, or museum.

13. Find a date to bring to an event.

14. Start dating a certain person.

15. Get married.

16. Get a divorce.

17. Save a marriage.

18. Break up another couple.

19. Get two other people to fall in love or get married.

20. Kidnap someone.

21. Escape from prison or captivity, or free a prisoner.

22. Throw a party.

23. Plan a successful wedding, festival, or charity gala.

24. Win a competition.

25. Procure top-secret information.

26. Run a marathon.

27. Become a soldier.

28. Have a baby.

29. Find a cure for a disease.

30. Develop a new invention.

31. Kick an addiction.

32. Overcome depression.

33. Recover from an illness or injury.

34. Become a better person.

35. Atone for a past wrong.

36. Find a particular object—magical, historical, or just plain valuable.

37. Destroy a particular object.

38. Become immortal.

39. Make new friends.

40. Reconcile with an estranged family member or former friend.

41. Find a missing person.

42. Go into hiding.

43. Change a law.

44. Bring peace to a region.

45. Become famous.

46. Start a small business, or save a business.

47. Own a house, or fix up an old house.

48. Create a happy holiday or summer vacation for their family.

49. Make contact with aliens.

50. Save a planet from destruction.

50 CONFLICTS TO A GOAL

Some of these conflicts are more external, and some of them are more internal. In many cases, "external" conflicts are only conflicts because of the character's feelings or beliefs about them.

1. Their lack of experience makes them doubt their ability to succeed.

2. Their history of failure makes them doubt their ability to succeed.

3. They have a physical health issue, a physical disadvantage, or an injury that is an impediment to achieving the goal.

4. They are lacking in money or equipment.

5. They have a tight deadline or a short window of opportunity; they don't have much time to get it done.

6. They fear it would be selfish to pursue this.

7. They fear other people will think they're selfish if they pursue this.

8. They fear other people will think they're arrogant if they pursue this.

9. Due to other responsibilities, they struggle to find the time to work on this.

10. They are in competition with a determined and talented rival.

11. They feel that they're not truly deserving of what they want.

12. They fear it's shallow or silly to want what they want.

13. A rival attempts to injure or kill them in order to keep them from achieving the goal.

14. A rival, family member, or friend sabotages their attempts to attain the goal.

15. They fear they'll make a fool of themselves by pursuing this goal, and people will laugh at them.

16. They fear they'll disappoint their parents by pursuing this path instead of another one.

17. The people on the team they have to work with are not talented, not committed, or a mix of both.

18. The team doesn't accept the main character as their leader.

19. The people on their designated team can't stop fighting with one another.

20. One or more family members, friends, or peers tell them they should give up because they don't have a chance.

21. Pursuing the goal will mean they neglect someone they love.

22. Pursuing the goal will put someone they love in danger.

23. They fear they've wasted too much time or money already in pursuit of this dream.

24. They fear they've invested too much time or money in another goal to switch to this one now.

25. As they pursue the goal, they run the risk of being expelled, fired, banished, imprisoned, or executed.

26. There's a warrant out for their arrest or a bounty for their capture.

27. They are imprisoned or confined.

28. They have a mental health issue that's an impediment to achieving this goal.

29. They fear they're too young or too old to succeed—or to even try.

30. Achieving the goal requires attending many meetings and navigating a lot of bureaucracy.

31. Achieving the goal requires a long journey.

32. The weather impedes them from achieving their goal.

33. They fear that pursuing the goal will make them look like a hypocrite due to things they've said or done in the past.

34. Achieving this goal will require deception or theft, and they see themselves as an honest person.

35. Pursuing this goal goes against their religious beliefs.

36. A dangerous creature, individual, or enemy force lies between them and their goal.

37. A small but pressing issue, or a side quest, tempts them to abandon or delay their mission.

38. They will have to ask for help to achieve this, which goes against their pride.

39. They'll have to start all over again as a complete beginner to achieve this, which goes against their pride.

40. They will have to ask for help from someone they dislike or from someone they wronged.

41. They will have to sacrifice something they also really want.

42. They lack a specific skill that's key to achieving the goal.

43. Pursuing the goal means facing a phobia such as public speaking or flying.

44. Their romantic partner opposes their dream, or is unconvinced that it's a good idea.

45. To achieve the goal, they must part ways with someone they love.

46. To achieve this goal, they'll have to betray someone.

47. The fact that they are human—or not human—poses a challenge.

48. They have to overcome a barrier—a social one, or a physical one.

49. A law or a lawsuit poses a challenge.

50. They struggle to overcome laziness or bad habits in order to pursue the goal.

50 CONFLICTS TO A ROMANCE

1. She told herself she'd never date someone of their profession or personality type again.

2. He told someone he'd only date someone of a certain personality type or in a certain life situation.

3. They live in different countries—or different planets—and will only be together for a short time.

4. One of them is dating or engaged to someone else.

5. She broke his heart in the past, so he struggles to trust her again.

6. Her last partner cheated on her or wronged her, so she doesn't trust romantic relationships in general.

7. She wronged someone he cared about in the past, so he struggles to forgive her—or refuses to hear her side of the story.

8. He did something very wrong in the past, so she finds it hard to believe that he's a better person now.

9. She's a suspect in a criminal investigation.

10. He believes she's already in a romantic relationship, although she's actually faking it.

11. Someone else is vying for his affections—and seems to be succeeding.

12. One particular person is attempting to keep them apart or thwart their attraction.

13. Their families hate each other.

14. They swore they were taking a break from dating.

15. She swore she'd never get into a serious romantic relationship, because she fears being controlled or tied down.

16. He believes he's bad at relationships and will only disappoint the other guy in the end.

17. One of them has to travel all the time for work.

18. One of them is deployed in the armed forces.

19. They're competing for the same job or championship.

20. One of them is determined to keep the other one from attaining their goal.

21. Their employer has a strict no-dating policy.

22. One of them is the boss of the other, so dating wouldn't be ethical.

23. One of them has a hard time being vulnerable or showing his emotions.

24. She believes she's too unattractive to be attractive to him.

25. He believes he's too strange or too awkward to be attractive to her.

26. She believes she's too old for romance, period.

27. He's a widower who believes you only have one soulmate.

28. She has a dangerous job that could put the other person at risk.

29. She has a demanding job or schedule, and it's hard to find time for a relationship.

30. They don't like any of the same things.

31. One of them is the bodyguard of the other, and dating is definitely not part of the job.

32. He's afraid that his friends would judge him for dating her.

33. One of them is hiding a dark secret.

34. One of them is hiding a secret identity.

35. They're of two different cultures, races, or species.

36. He's mortal, and she's immortal.

37. One of them is non-corporeal—a ghost or a spirit, for instance.

38. She could be imprisoned, banished, or executed for dating someone of his kind.

39. One of them has taken the other captive.

40. They're on opposing sides of a dispute or lawsuit.

41. They're on opposing sides of a war.

42. One of them is staid and predictable, while the other is impulsive.

43. One of them is a workaholic, while the other is lazy or lacking in ambition.

44. One of them is cheery and optimistic, while the other is cynical.

45. Being with him would require a sacrifice, such as giving up a dream job or moving far away from her family.

46. She believes no one will want to date her because she's a single mom.

47. He believes no one will want to date him because of his physical or mental illness or disability.

48. They're good friends, and she doesn't want to risk ruining their friendship by taking it to the next level.

49. They're good friends, and he's positive she could never see him as anything more.

50. They both made terrible first impressions on one another.

50 REASONS FOR CHARACTERS TO FALL IN LOVE (BESIDES GOOD LOOKS)

When I edit romance novel manuscripts and manuscripts with a romance subplot, I sometimes ask authors in the margins: "Why do they like each other?" Readers become more emotionally invested in the fictional relationship when there's more to it than physical attraction, and "there's just something about them" often doesn't cut it. If you know why your characters fall in love with each other, and there's a clear conflict to the romance, you've got a strong foundation for a good love story.

1. The character shares an unusual hobby or passion with the protagonist.

2. The character is polite and dignified.

3. They're a loveable goofball.

4. They make hilarious jokes.

5. They're the only one who seems to get the protagonist's jokes.

6. They're shy…and your protagonist thinks it's adorable.

7. They're extroverted, making friends wherever they go…and your protagonist admires that.

8. The character shares an unusual background or past experience with the protagonist.

10. The character shares a rare ability with the protagonist.

11. The character shares a fringe point of view with the protagonist.

12. The character and the protagonist are both fighting for the same near-hopeless cause.

13. The protagonist is impressed by the character's faith.

14. The protagonist is impressed by how hard-working the character is.

15. The character has a sexy voice.

16. They're positive and encouraging.

17. They say things that make the protagonist see life in a new way.

18. They're extremely intelligent.

19. They're fun to have an intellectual debate with.

20. They're not only wealthy, but generous.

21. They can light up a whole room with their smile.

22. They're kind to the protagonist's child, pet, or eccentric relative.

23. They're confident.

24. They're intense and mysterious.

25. They do an act of kindness.

26. They confront a bully.

27. They don't judge the protagonist for something that others might.

28. They call the protagonist on their nonsense.

29. They compliment the protagonist.

30. They make an ordinary night into an adventure.

31. They take risks, which the protagonist finds exciting.

32. They understand the protagonist without needing a lengthy explanation.

33. They have an amazing sense of personal style.

34. They wear a uniform.

35. They stay calm in a crisis.

36. They work well as a team with the protagonist on a challenge.

37. They're honest.

38. They do what they say they're going to do.

39. They make sure the protagonist is comfortable.

40. They make sure the protagonist is safe.

41. They're an incredible cook.

42. They're an amazing kisser.

43. They give fantastic backrubs.

44. They seem like they'll be a good parent.

45. Like the protagonist, they prefer to be child-free.

46. Like the protagonist, they're a homebody.

47. Like the protagonist, they want to travel the world.

48. They share the protagonist's moral values.

49. They don't mind that the protagonist isn't a big talker.

50. They're someone that the protagonist can talk to for hours and hours.

25 REASONS TO JOIN A DANGEROUS QUEST OR BATTLE

When the action is likely to lead to struggle, injury, or death, the motivation needs to be especially clear. If you have a group of characters going on an adventure or fighting together, each character might have a different motivation.

1. They want to be one of the first humans or the first of their kind… to travel to a certain place, achieve a certain thing, serve as an officer, or triumph in battle.

2. They want to be seen as a great adventurer or a hero.

3. They were already enlisted in the armed forces, or already in service; although they didn't expect to fight a war or go on a dangerous quest, it's their duty.

4. They've been conscripted, and they'll be imprisoned or shot if they refuse.

5. They want their would-be partner, their partner, their family, or their friends to be proud of them.

6. Their friends or family members are doing it, and the character wants to go with them and watch out for them.

7. Their friends or family members are doing it, or their forebears did it, so the character figures it must be the right thing to do.

8. The character has failed in other ways in the past, and the quest or war is a path to redemption.

9. They are part of the ruling family or a ruling class, and they believe it's their duty.

10. They want to save their country or their world.

11. They want to protect their loved ones.

12. They've secured a favor for someone else in exchange for them going on the quest or fighting in the war.

13. They want to punish someone for past wrongs, on a personal or a national level.

14. They are motivated by bigotry and hatred for another group of people.

15. They believe that something should rightfully belong to them or to their nation.

16. They believe a successful quest or a military victory will lead to higher social standing, or even immense power.

17. They believe a successful quest or a military victory will lead to riches.

18. They're a soldier of fortune, hired for this particular war or quest.

19. They've never had the opportunity or means to travel, and they want to see the wide world.

20. Because of a special skill or a particular situation, they know they have more chance of succeeding than anyone else, so they feel obligated.

21. A trusted authority figure convinced them to do it, for one of many reasons on this list.

22. They have been brainwashed or enchanted into believing they must do it.

23. A dream or a divine messenger told them that they must do it.

24. They have a death wish, and no one would think badly of them for dying as a result of this quest or battle.

25. They have secret plans to sabotage the army or the group.

25 WAYS TO MAKE A QUEST OR BATTLE MORE DIFFICULT

1. Someone has new reason to doubt the cause.

2. Someone has new reason to doubt their own ability.

3. Someone has lost a magical ability.

4. They needed to be incognito or undercover, and someone has been recognized.

5. Someone's past misdeeds or true identity are revealed, causing conflict within the group.

6. A valuable member of the company has quit or gone missing.

7. Two members of the same company both feel they should be in charge, leading to a lack of clear direction.

8. Members of the same company quarrel, leading to an unwillingness to help one another, defection, or even violence.

9. They reach more treacherous terrain.

10. They have a scarcity or lack of food or water.

11. A wild animal attacks them.

12. Someone loses their weapon or runs out of ammunition.

13. A thief steals all their stuff.

14. Someone gets sick.

15. Someone gets injured.

16. Someone commits a crime during the course of the adventure, and now they're a fugitive.

17. Someone gets captured.

18. Someone gets cursed or enchanted.

19. A companion is killed, leaving them grieving.

20. Someone has received tragic news from back home.

21. The enemy's ranks have grown.

22. The enemy has created a powerful new weapon.

23. A location they expected to be a safe harbor is now anything but.

24. Due to a change in circumstances, they now have to get somewhere or do something twice as quickly as they originally planned.

25. They get hopelessly lost.

75 WAYS TO RESIST OR OVERTHROW AN EVIL REGIME

This list is for writers of dystopian fiction, speculative fiction, and fantasy. Your characters might want to overthrow alien overlords, topple a monarchy, or resist the rise of fascism or corporatocracy. At the very least, they may want to make the regime less efficient, demoralize its most loyal servants, and save some people from harm. However, they might be at an enormous disadvantage in terms of people, training, and resources.

To develop this list, I relied heavily on the excellent *Simple Sabotage Field Manual*, developed by the CIA in the United States to train citizens to sabotage German Nazism. I also researched resistance movements, revolutions, and wars in global history. Some strategies are only appropriate for technologically advanced societies, and some strategies are more appropriate for resisting a rising power rather than an entrenched one. This list ranges from nonviolent protest and petty acts of sabotage to classic tactics of guerilla and traditional warfare.

1. Identify like-minded resisters and meet regularly in secret in order to strategize, possibly under the guise of another purpose, such as a hiking club or a charitable nonprofit.

2. Develop codes or private, secure channels for communication between rebels.

3. With family members, friends, teachers, coworkers, neighbors, or other associates, speak out against positive comments about the regime, sowing seeds of doubt if possible.

4. Praise former loyalists for expressing doubt of the regime, placing the blame for their past loyalty on the regime's deceptiveness.

5. Shout at government officials in collusion with the dictator or oppressive government at town halls, meetings, and public appearances.

6. Make public speeches that appeal to traditional values, religious values, or revered historical figures from the past.

7. Make public speeches that delineate the ways that the regime is harming the citizens or countrymen it pretends to support.

8. Deface or tear down propaganda such as statues, signs, and posters.

9. Post anti-regime signs and posters or online propaganda.

10. Distribute flyers, pamphlets, and books to stoke revolutionary sentiments.

11. Document and distribute detailed reports of the regime's wrongdoings.

12. Ruin official speeches and events with memorable distractions designed to embarrass the regime.

13. Stage protests of the regime at central locations, high-profile events, government buildings, prisons, and detention or internment camps.

14. Combine protests with concerts, circuses, street performers, or visual spectacles to attract more participants.

15. Create popular songs, artwork, plays, poems, novels, and movies decrying or satirizing the regime.

16. Hold vigils for the persecuted, imprisoned, or disappeared, with candles, religious rituals, prayers, or public speakers.

17. Honor the dead through public funeral or memorial services, processions, and motorcades, with or without a body or bodies.

18. Stage walkouts from schools and businesses.

19. Create a new name, a new slogan, a new symbol, and/or a signature color or item of clothing that gives members of the resistance a shared sense of identity and belonging.

20. Distract the regime and dilute their propaganda by raising public outcry about previously ignored issues.

21. Identify and boycott the businesses that are most supportive of the regime.

22. Develop a real-life or online persona that allows one to infiltrate groups of loyalists, gain their trust, and sow seeds of doubt and rebellion.

23. Develop a real-life or online persona that allows one to befriend or date high-ranking officials and learn about secret plans.

24. Posing as a loyalist, take a job with the regime in order to document its activities and/or sabotage it from within.

25. Spread rumors that erode the trust between high-ranking members of the regime, making them suspect one another.

26. Tempt high-ranking officials into disloyalty by convincing them it'll make them richer and more powerful.

27. Publicly identify hooded executioners or other secret collaborators, sharing their names, photographs or physical likenesses, and addresses.

28. Identify the locations of the regime's secret offices, bunkers, storage facilities, camps, or prisons, in order to observe closely, attack directly, or publicize widely.

29. Shun and shame the regime's bureaucrats, police force, soldiers, and collaborators, coming up with new names for them and harassing them on or off duty.

30. Refuse to serve or rent to the regime's officials and soldiers. If necessary for personal safety, feign other reasons: the kitchen at the

restaurant is closed due to faulty equipment; the apartment is being remodeled.

31. Report the regime's bureaucrats, soldiers, and collaborators for minor infractions of the law.

32. Make false anonymous reports to waste the regime's time and overload their systems.

33. Misfile or mislabel reports.

34. Misspell names and key words in official orders and government reports.

35. Make the regime less efficient by delaying the delivery of mail, "forgetting" to respond to a message, or forwarding a message to the wrong person.

36. Delay following the orders of the regime by asking for clarifications, waiting for a certain person to come back to work, obtaining a necessary permit, or waiting for a certain system upgrade for better security. Pretend to be busy complying while doing nothing.

37. Take advantage of existing social media algorithms and proven social media strategies to amplify reports of injustice and calls for soldiers to defect.

38. Organize workers' strikes.

39. Secretly offer shelter to people hunted by the regime. Read *The Diary of Anne Frank* and the history of the German resistance for examples.

40. Obtain false identification documents for people hunted by the regime.

41. Provide food, supplies, and medical attention to people harmed by the regime.

42. Provide safe passage to those who need to escape the region or country. The history of the Underground Railroad in the United States offers good inspiration.

43. Arrange a hornet, scorpion, or rat infestation in the regime's palace or key government buildings.

44. Disrupt a government building's wifi signal by deploying several wifi jammers attached to frequently moving targets, such as small AI-powered robots or rats let loose in the walls.

45. Sabotage the plumbing or sewage system in the regime's palace or the soldiers' barracks.

46. Block the chimneys of a castle or royal residence so it fills with smoke in the winter.

47. Compromise a government building's electrical system so it loses power.

48. Compromise the transportation of the regime: cut straps on the saddles of horses, mix sugar or salt water with the gasoline in the fuel tanks of trucks, or hack the spacecraft.

49. Destroy government records or valuable supplies by triggering the sprinkler system.

50. Orchestrate a cyberattack that destroys the regime's records or exposes their secrets.

51. Conduct a cyberattack that alters, stalls, or crashes the regime's digital systems.

52. Start fires in the palace or government buildings and the buildings the rulers rely on, particularly those that already contain flammable or explosive material, such as barns full of hay or grain, textile mills, airplane hangars, munitions factories, oil refineries, boat docks and marinas, chemical plants, warehouses used to store chemicals, and space stations.

53. Remove street signs, change the signs in front of buildings, or alter maps to confuse an occupying force.

54. Make a road needed by the regime impassable: for instance, stage an "accident" with a truck, causing a big spill, or secretly damage a levee so the road is flooded.

55. Harm or destroy bridges or train tracks heavily used by the regime.

56. Befriend other groups, foreign or domestic, who have common cause against the regime.

57. Secretly stockpile weapons, ammunition, food, water, sanitary supplies, and medical supplies to prepare for conflict.

58. Purchase and hoard or distribute large quantities of supplies or goods needed by the regime or its armies.

59. Train for traditional warfare, such as hand-to-hand combat; fighting with swords, crossbows, or guns; field medicine and surgery; driving trucks or tanks; piloting airplanes, helicopters, unmanned drones, or spaceships.

60. Develop skills for biological warfare. In a novel set in a world that's not technologically advanced, two examples are the Golden Horde's use of cadavers at the Siege of Caffa and the use of smallpox-infected blankets in the French and Indian War. In a technologically advanced world, biological agents might have a long incubation period that makes it impossible to investigate how or why it was deployed, or it may be impervious to existing methods of detection.

61. Develop skills for cyberwarfare, such as hacking digital systems and poisoning AI data sets.

62. Create a virtual reality game that serves as training for insurgents.

63. Target and assassinate plainclothes intelligence agents and police officers, intimidating people to resign. As an example, read about Michael Collins, the Irish Republican Army, and the Squad.

64. Target and assassinate government officials and vocal opponents of the revolution. For examples, read about Communist insurgents in Vietnam and the Basque separatist movement ETA in Spain.

65. Carry out an attack or a fake attack or atrocity while disguised as soldiers of the regime.

66. Feign friendship, enter a fortified target, and attack from within. For a remarkable example, read about the Ojibwe attack on Fort Michilimackinac in 1763.

67. Ambush a small group of soldiers during a convoy or patrol in a location that provides ample cover for the insurgents.

68. Surround a vulnerable target and attack at first light. Withdraw if insurgent casualties are sustained. Repeat.

69. Use troop movements or false reports to confuse the enemy and gain the element of surprise, as General George Washington did in the American Revolutionary War.

70. Dress a dead person as an officer, plant fake battle plans on their person, and put them in a place where the enemy will find them. As an example, read about Operation Mincemeat, a British subterfuge in the Second World War.

71. Convert fishing boats, sailboats, cruise ships, or yachts into disguised warships.

72. Capture enemy ships, continue to fly the enemy's flag, and use them for surprise attacks.

73. Through a coordinated campaign of misinformation or manipulation of digital systems, lead two factions of the enemy army to mistake one another for rebels and attack one another.

74. Lure the enemy into a dangerous situation or into dangerous terrain. One example: at the Battle of the Trebbia River, Hannibal baited the Roman infantry into crossing a freezing river, leaving them cold and shivering. Another example: in the naval Battle of Myeongnyang, the Korean admiral Yi Sun-sin, going to battle with thirteen ships, lured three hundred Japanese ships into a narrow strait with strong currents. When the tide shifted, the currents pushed the ships backwards, and some crashed into each other.

75. Create shock and panic among the enemy's ranks by introducing a new element to a battle. Hannibal's elephants are a classic example.

50 KINDS OF MAGICAL SPELLS

If you're writing fantasy or paranormal stories, you might want to work some magic into it. You might have ordinary characters working with spells, charms, and incantations, or the magic may only work for a natural witch, magician, or other person with magical powers. A character may be casting spells for good, for neutral purposes, or for evil.

To create this list of spells for witchcraft and wizardry, I drew extensively from ancient magic (including Latin spells, African spells, Celtic magic, Jewish magic, and more), but also from literature, modern Wiccan spells, and popular culture.

Many spells involve chants and incantations, sometimes from a spell book. Your character may also know secret words and phrases about magic, in esoteric languages, or they may know someone's true name.

As far as the other elements of a spell go: it's up to you as a writer! In folklore and tradition, magic has involved any or several of the following;

drawing magical circles or symbols

stones and gems

plants, herbs, and oils

specially created potions and powders

jewelry, amulets, and charms

masks

animal pelts and/or horns worn on the head

candles

burning or breaking objects

burning or burying words written on paper

burying or hiding objects

jar spells and charm bags—putting several magical ingredients, such as herbs or crystals, in a jar, small bottle, or bag to carry with you or keep nearby

certain foods and drinks

hair, blood, and bones

ritual bathing

ritual singing

ritual drumming

ritual dancing

enchanted tools such as wands and knives

enchanted objects

magical places, human-built or natural

aid from animals (sometimes called "familiars")

aid from spirits, magical beings, demons (if they're doing "black magic"), or deities

poppets, "voodoo dolls," or wax or carved figures (or photographs, in a modern story)

magical timing (such as midnight, a full moon, an equinox or solstice, a holiday, or an eclipse)

sacrifice (from a drop or two of blood, to an animal sacrifice, to a human sacrifice for your truly evil villains)

Here are fifty types of magical spells you can include in your story!

1. Love potions, love spells, and obsession spells. Be careful how you use spells for love in a romance plot; it's not romantic if one person has no choice.

2. attraction spells (less serious than love spells, but the same note above applies)

3. beauty spells

4. "glamour" spells that create any illusion of a different appearance

5. money spells

6. fame spells

7. happiness spells

8. success spells

9. new job spells

10. power spells to gain a promotion or a greater sphere of influence

11. protection in battle spells—this can be an invisible shield spell, or it can render the warrior invincible

12. spells to disarm an opponent

13. general protection spells

14. healing spells. In a few stories, "white magic" healing spells involve taking the pain from the other person onto oneself.

15. spells to ward off disease or pestilence

16. spells to cause disease or sickness in another person

17. spells to cause someone to drop dead

18. spells to knock someone unconscious or "freeze" them

19. sleeping spells

20. safe travels spells

21. good luck in gambling spells

22. general good luck spells

23. bad luck spells for others

24. spells to cause an enemy to be killed in battle

25. spells to find what's lost

26. psychokinesis spells to move objects or make them fly through the air

27. memory spells—for remembering or forgetting

28. rain spells to end drought

29. spells to cause natural disasters—tsunamis, hurricanes

30. spells to set things on fire (or to send balls of fire at an opponent, if used as a dueling spell)

31. alchemy spells (turning lead to gold, for instance)

32. binding spells—these don't harm a person, but they prevent a person from doing harm

33. banishing spells, for people or for any negative influence

34. karma spells, so that people will reap the positive or negative benefits of their actions quickly

35. justice spells for fair outcomes to trials

36. protection spells against hexes and curses

37. hex-breaking or curse reversal spells

38. exorcism spells to cast out ghosts and demons

39. spells to summon a magical or supernatural being, such as a ghost, demon, fairy, or magical animal

40. spells to communicate with the dead

41. spells to get other people or animals to do your bidding

42. spells to create a living creature, such as the homunculus in alchemy and the golem in Jewish folklore

43. fertility spells

44. spells to open locks and doors

45. spells to create light in dark places

46. persuasion spells to convince someone of something or win them over

47. spells to read someone's mind or go into their psyche

48. spells to enter the body of another person or animal, or trade bodies with them

49. divination spells to see into the future

50. blessing spells for homes, marriages, or individuals

50 MOTIVES FOR MURDER

In most murder mysteries, a few different characters have plausible motives for committing the murder. In fact, a couple of mystery writers have told me they start with these motives when plotting their story. Of course, your sleuth's guess at a motive may turn out to be false.

Keep in mind that in some cases, the death may be the accidental outcome of an assault (manslaughter). In rare cases, the victim may have been mistaken for the actual intended target.

1. the victim was a witness to a crime committed by the murderer or someone close to the murderer

2. the victim's testimony put the murderer or someone close to the murderer in prison

3. the victim threatened to reveal a damaging personal secret about the murderer

4. the victim had a history of bullying the murderer or someone close to them

5. the victim had a history of physically abusing the murderer or someone close to them

6. the murderer killed the victim in order to rob them

7. the murderer killed the victim in order to inherit their money and/or property

8. the murderer killed the victim in order to get a life insurance payout

9. the murderer killed the victim in order to collect their disability check

10. the murderer killed the victim for ending their friendship

11. the murderer killed someone for forbidding them to see their romantic crush

12. the victim spurned the murderer's romantic overtures

13. the victim was romantically unfaithful or believed to be unfaithful to the murderer

14. the victim's spouse wanted to be free of them, without the cost and/or stigma of divorce

15. the victim threatened the murderer with a romantic breakup or divorce

16. the murderer was jealous of their ex-romantic partner's new relationship

17. the murderer was upset about the pregnancy of their romantic partner, secret lover, or family member

18. the murderer was jealous of their romantic partner's attention to a new baby

19. the murderer wanted to pretend the victim's baby was their own

20. the murderer wanted full custody of their child, so they killed their ex-partner

21. the murderer perceived a family member as needing an extraordinary amount of caretaking

22. the murderer believed they were doing the victim a favor, due to the perceived suffering of the victim

23. the murderer didn't like the victim's politics

24. the murderer didn't like the victim's religion

25. the murderer didn't like the victim's gender or sexual orientation

26. the victim was a professional rival whom the murderer wished to eliminate

27. the murderer killed a boss who fired them

28. the victim wronged the murderer's family member

28. a cult or gang leader persuaded the murderer to kill in order to be part of the group

29. the victim refused to loan the murderer money

30. the murderer owed a large amount of money to the victim and couldn't or didn't want to pay

31. the murderer killed a police officer to avoid arrest

32. the murderer killed a guard to get out of prison or help a loved one get out of prison

33. the victim was a kidnapper, and the person they abducted killed them in order to get free

34. the murderer killed someone close to them in order to receive sympathy as a grieving parent, child, or spouse

35. the murder sexually assaulted the victim and didn't want them to report it

36. the murderer and the victim had a property dispute

37. the murderer wanted to take credit for the victim's creative work or invention

38. the murderer wanted to steal the victim's identity

39. road rage: the victim cut them off on the highway or bumped into the back of their car

40. the murderer believed the victim ruined their wedding, graduation, or holiday celebration

41. the murderer wasn't invited to the victim's wedding or party

---

42. the murderer was mentally ill and heard voices telling them to commit the murder

43. the murderer was mentally ill and believed the victim was a demon or another person in disguise

44. the murderer believed the victim had brought shame or dishonor on their family

45. the murderer believed the victim's business venture would do harm to the environment

46. the murderer was angry that the victim, their partner, refused to let a family member or friend in need live with them

47. the victim destroyed or disposed of something irreplaceable that belonged to the murderer, such as a family heirloom or a social media account with a large following

48. the murderer wanted to look like a hero, so they attempted to arrange a near death that they could "rescue" the victim from

49. the murderer was hired to kill the victim, for a reason listed above

50. the murderer was framing someone else for murder, for a reason listed above

100 MURDER WEAPONS

When it comes to stabbing, strangling, or especially blunt force, the options are almost limitless. I'm including a few real-life examples of administering poisons. Virtually all poisons can be detected by a forensic toxicologist in a contemporary murder investigation, but poisoners could still get away with it if the death is assumed to have been of natural causes, if it appears to have been an recreational drug overdose, or if it appears to have been an accidental poisoning, such as a fatal allergy. In the past, poisoning was much more difficult to prove.

Hit men and mobsters sometimes left their guns, which were difficult to trace back to the shooter, at the scene of the crime. That way, they wouldn't be caught in possession of the weapon. In some cases, murder may be staged as a suicide.

1. hands (punching; strangling)

2. feet

3. elbows

4. handgun

5. rifle

6. antique pistol

7. bow and arrow

8. kitchen knife

9. Swiss Army knife

10. sword

11. spear

12. barbecue fork

13. skewer

14. screwdriver

15. scissors

16. rotary cutter (used by quilters)

17. pitchfork

18. ice pick

19. broken bottle

20. glass from broken window or door

21. garden shears

22. axe

23. machete

24. chainsaw

25. table saw

26. shovel

27. metal chair

28. hammer

29. crowbar

30. tire iron

31. iron skillet

32. clothes iron

33. golf club

34. fireplace poker

35. decorative statue

36. dumbbell or kettle ball

37. baseball bat

38. brick

39. rock (blunt force, or larger rock dropped on victim)

40. walking stick

41. pantyhose (strangling)

42. scarf or necktie (strangling)

43. piano wire

44. guitar string

45. chain

46. electrical cord

47. belt

48. rope (strangling or hanging)

49. car or truck

50. motorcycle

51. train (pushing victim in front of or off it)

52. heavy traffic (pushing victim into it)

53. balcony, roof, or ledge (pushing victim off it)

54. ladder (tipping it over when the victim's on it)

55. boat (pushing victim off it, in the middle of the ocean)

56. plane or helicopter (pushing victim out of it)

57. subzero temperatures (leaving victim in wilderness, in light clothing)

58. deep freezer (locking victim into it)

59. fire

60. Molotov cocktail or other IED (improvised explosive device)

61. grenade

62. swimming pool

63. bathtub or hot tub

64. kitchen or bathroom sink (drowning)

65. toilet (drowning)

66. antifreeze, added to food or drink

67. thallium, added to food, drink, or table salt

68. strychnine, in capsules emptied of a prescribed drug

69. paraquat

70. rat poison

71. crushed peanuts or peanut butter, added to the food of someone with a serious peanut allergy

72. lobster or shrimp, added to the food of someone with a serious shellfish allergy

73. fentanyl, added to recreational drugs

74. hemlock

75. monkshood (*aconitum napellus,* also called wolfsbane*)*

76. foxglove

77. belladonna or deadly nightshade

78. arsenic

---

79. cyanide, found in bitter almonds (and sometimes made into a paste)

80. deathstalker or Palestine yellow scorpion—the sting could kill a child, an elderly person, or a person with a heart condition

81. venomous snake, such as saw-scaled viper

82. dog, sicced on the victim

83. horse—causing the horse a victim is riding to rear or bolt

84. hippopotamus—victim pushed into zoo enclosure, or pushed out of car or boat in the hippo's habitat. Hippos kill about five hundred people every year.

85. lamp

86. flashlight

87. knitting needle

88. sock full of loose change or batteries

89. paperweight

90. wrench

91. metal water bottle

92. pillow (smothering)

93. paper cutter

94. coat stand

95. vat of deep-frying oil

96. locked door (hunger/thirst)

97. rock climbing or skydiving gear (sabotaging equipment)

98. stiletto heel

99. cutting board

100. rolling pin

100 MURDER CLUES

Amateur sleuths and seasoned investigators alike use clues to establish motive, means, and opportunity, and ultimately to solve the mystery. These may be obtained through crime scene investigations, searches (from online searches, to rifling through a suspect's or victim's trash), conversations (including formal questioning and casual chitchat), and surveillance.

Some clues may lead to other clues. For instance, a key may lead to a clue in a safety deposit box. And of course, in a mystery story, not all "clues" lead to the guilty party! Misdirects or "red herrings" often make the sleuth—and the reader—suspect someone who's innocent.

1. an email

2. a text

3. a handwritten letter

4. a journal entry

5. a high school yearbook

6. a personal note or list

7. the impression left by a pen on a pad of paper, after the written-on sheet has been torn off

8. a bill or invoice

9. a receipt

10. a tax return

11. an electronic payment

12. a bank account. A recently opened, closed, or drained bank account can be a clue, and so can large or irregular deposits or withdrawals.

13. an insurance policy

A new or increased policy on a person or a building may provide a plausible motive.

14. a significant debt—gambling, business, credit card, medical, or school loans

15. pill bottles or a drug stash

16. a will

17. a marriage license

18. a birth or adoption certificate

19. divorce paperwork

20. a business contract

21. a falling-out with another person or a group

22. a history of animosity

23. a past arrest or fine

24. a past breakup

25. a past job loss

26. a clandestine meeting

27. an illicit affair

28. a secretive visit to a certain building

29. a train ticket

30. a boarding pass

31. a hasty move to another address, city, or country

32. a package

---

33. signs of disturbance or desecration at a gravesite

34. a movie, theater, or concert ticket

35. a brochure or flyer

36. a magazine or newspaper clipping

37. a recently and/or secretly set up profile on a dating app

38. a photo or video clip

This may show two unexpected people together or show someone in an unexpected context. A noise or detail in the background may be a clue hidden in plain sight.

39. security camera footage

40. food in the fridge

41. a food delivery

42. the contents of the murder victim's stomach

43. a food or candy wrapper

44. a recently purchased book (or recently checked out library book)

45. an underlined passage in a book

46. a building permit

47. a blueprint

48. a job or school application

49. an advertisement for an open job position

50. internet search history

51. posts and comments on social media

52. a guest list or invitation

53. a key

54. a mask

55. a uniform

56. a costume

57. a tattoo

58. lipstick on a tissue, handkerchief, or collar

59. blood stains

60. food or beverage stains

61. mud or dirt on shoes or clothing

62. rips in clothing

63. mud on tires or the interior of a vehicle

64. scratches or damage to a door, a vehicle, or a boat

65. scratches, bruises, injuries, or a new limp

66. a broken stair rail or fence

67. a broken window or door

68. footprints

69. fingerprints

70. tire tracks

71. a prescription or order for a medical test

72. a person gone missing

73. a pet gone missing

74. a vehicle gone missing

75. a missing license plate

76. an ingredient used to make an explosive in the suspect's garage

77. a poisonous substance in the suspect's garage or medicine chest

78. the purchase of items used for restraint, such as rope, duct tape, or zip ties

79. a gun or knife in the suspect's possession

80. a parking ticket

81. a suspect's particular skill or training, such as hunting or martial arts

82. the scent of a certain cologne or perfume

83. the smell of gasoline or bleach

84. the hiring of a cleaning or sanitization service

85. a name change

86. a hair color and/or hairstyle change

87. an unpublished manuscript or screenplay

88. a poem, song lyrics, or a playlist

89. a burner phone

90. a suspect's unusual level of interest in the investigation

91. a child or pet who's terrified of a suspect

92. an item of the victim's in the suspect's possession

93. a piece of jewelry

94. a discarded article of clothing

95. clothing fibers

96. a fingernail

97. a hair

98. a bone

99. evidence from a DNA testing site

100. the past untimely death of someone else associated with the suspect

25 REASONS TO MOVE
TO A NEW TOWN

Leo Tolstoy once said, "All great literature is one of two stories; a man goes on a journey or a stranger comes to town." I don't think this is exactly true, but there are many wonderful books and movies about these two things, and many manuscripts I edit feature a character who's new in town. That's why I created a list of reasons to move, and you could also write about the journey there.

1. They're going to college in this new town. They might be a foreign exchange student.

2. They just landed a new job there, or their company transferred him to this office.

3. Their fiancé or spouse got a job there.

4. They're looking for a new job. For their occupation, this is the place to be.

5. They think this town is the perfect place to start a bed and breakfast, coffee shop, or other business.

6. Even though they're from a small town, they've always dreamed of life in the big city.

7. Even though they were born and raised in a bustling metropolis, they've always fantasized about an idyllic life in the country.

8. The character's aging parents live there, and the character is moving close by to look after them.

9. The character's siblings or parents live there, and they're a single parent who could use more help with the kids.

10. They want to be near their nieces, nephews, or grandkids.

11. They want to get far away from their unbearable family.

12. One of their parents or grandparents died, and they're moving back to her hometown to get the house ready for sale—or maybe live in it.

13. They moved after being involved in a terrible scandal or a crime. Maybe they even changed their name.

14. They moved after a painful breakup. There's no avoiding their ex in that little town!

15. Something awful happened to them, and the move will help them put all those terrible memories behind them.

16. They think this is a better place to raise their kids.

17. They're sick of living in a cramped apartment and want to live somewhere where they can afford a house.

18. They feel as though they'll never meet their soulmate in that tiny hometown—or in that snobbish suburb.

19. They've had it with winter. They were made for this sunny climate.

20. They won't be there forever, but they have a temporary work assignment such as an environmental study, a consulting gig, or a political campaign.

21. They won't be there forever, but they've rented out a beach cottage or city loft for the summer to work on a project or enjoy a sabbatical.

22. The character or their child is sick and needs to be closer to a particular hospital or treatment center.

23. They just needed a shorter commute. They were tired of driving in from the neighboring town.

24. They saw this unusual home on a real estate site and just fell in love with it.

25. They used to live there, as a kid, a student, or a young man, and they always regretted moving away.

25 REASONS TO STAY IN A DIFFICULT RELATIONSHIP

If your character is in a terrible romantic relationship, readers will be very quick to ask, "Why don't they just leave?"—unless they understand the character's motivation.

Of course, the character may have several motivations on this list. Some of these motivations may be exaggerated or needless fears. Some items on this list might also be applicable to someone staying in a bad roommate situation, a bad job, or a toxic friendship or family relationship.

1. After devoting many years to this relationship, the character doesn't want to feel as though those years were wasted.

2. The relationship used to be fun, and the character is hoping it can get that way again. Maybe they still have a good time once in a great while.

3. The character believes that they are going through a rough patch due to extenuating circumstances, and that both the circumstances and the relationship can improve.

4. Their partner has promised that they will change or make things better. Maybe they've been sober recently, or they've started going to therapy.

5. Family members or friends might judge the character harshly for ending the relationship.

6. The whole community might judge them harshly for ending the relationship.

7. In a breakup, the character is likely to lose their good relationships with the partner's family or with mutual friends. Their friend group might take the partner's side.

8. The character is afraid of being alone and lonely. They may think they are too weird, too unattractive, too poor, or too old to attract a better partner, or any partner.

9. The character or their partner can't afford an apartment on their own. Maybe they don't have the training or experience to get a job that would pay the bills.

10. The character or their partner is dependent on their partner's health insurance.

11. A divorce or split might be hard on the children.

12. A divorce settlement might mean either limited access to the children or little financial help in raising them.

13. If the character divorces, they will have to pay alimony to their ex, which will be more expensive than staying in the relationship.

14. The couple and/or their families have spent a lot of money on the upcoming or recent wedding, and everyone has congratulated them. Breaking things off will be a poor return on everyone's financial and emotional investment.

15. The character wants kids, and they feel like they're getting to an age where it's not going to happen if they break up and try to start over with someone else.

16. The couple's intimate life is still satisfying, even though everything else is bad.

17. The relationship or the partner's behavior got worse very gradually, so it was difficult for the character to identify the point at which it became untenable.

18. Breaking up and being honest with everyone about the reason would mean revealing something about themselves that many people might find hard to accept. The character might even struggle to accept this about themselves.

19. The character believes all relationships are this bad—because someone has told them "marriage is hard" and "life isn't perfect," or because they grew up around unhealthy relationships.

20. A relative of the partner employs the character.

21. It would be more difficult or impossible for the character to stay in that particular country if they divorced their partner, who is a natural-born citizen.

22. The character fears that if they leave, their partner will be devastated and may even harm themselves. Maybe their partner has even threatened to do this if they leave.

23. Due to the laws of the country or the power of their partner, they will be imprisoned, banished, or executed if they try to leave.

24. The character is afraid that if they leave, their partner will track them down and kill them. Maybe their partner has threatened this.

25. The character is afraid that if they leave, their partner will harm their family members. Again, maybe their partner has threatened to do so.

25 REASONS TO BREAK UP WITH SOMEONE

Maybe your character got out of a bad relationship; maybe their heart was broken when they got dumped. I've tried to list common reasons for breakups. In my own opinion, most of these are very good reasons to end a relationship, but some are not. In this list, "the character" refers to the one who takes the initiative to break things off, but the person who does that may be more of a villain in your story. Although I'm using the word "partner," this list can be used for less committed relationships.

1. The partner is physically abusive.

2. The partner is unfaithful.

3. The partner wants to be able to date other people when the relationship was previously exclusive.

4. The partner flirts with and compliments other people, or has a close relationship with another person that seems a little more than platonic—even though the partner swears that it is.

5. The partner has a hot temper and/or unpredictable emotional meltdowns.

6. The partner habitually speaks to the character with disrespect or contempt.

7. The character feels like they have to do too much of the work in the relationship. The duties could include working at a job, managing the finances, cleaning and cooking, raising the children, taking care of pets, making and keeping track of appointments, maintaining their joint relationships with friends and family, and/or making all the romantic plans and overtures.

8. Being a parent is overwhelming to the character. A divorce with joint custody would mean that they could get a few days a week to themselves.

9. The couple's parenting styles are incompatible, leading to many arguments.

10. The couple has incompatible approaches to finances. Maybe the partner is driving them into financial ruin, or has already done so.

11. The partner develops an addiction, their addiction gets worse, or their addiction causes a situation that makes the character decide that enough is enough.

12. The partner has gotten into legal trouble.

13. The partner adopts views on politics or religion that are abhorrent to the character.

14. The partner has new or worsening physical or mental health issues that make life more difficult or less fun for the character. In some cases, the character may hold the partner responsible for their health issues.

15. The partner has undergone a personality shift that most people would see as positive—they've become more ambitious, more confident, or more philanthropic—and it's disrupted the couple's dynamic.

16. The partner hasn't changed in the way the character expected. For instance, the partner is still partying like a college student, wearing quirky outfits, or indulging in their frivolous hobby.

17. The partner has new demands or expectations that the character finds unreasonable.

18. In the character's opinion, the partner doesn't want to spend enough time together. They're always busy at work or always studying; they prioritize friend hangouts over date nights. There could be a good reason why the partner has less time: for instance, studying for the LSAT, or looking after an ailing relative.

19. The character's friend or family member persuades them that the partner isn't good enough for them. For example, maybe the character is advised to find someone who is from their same cultural background, who doesn't have a child from a previous marriage, or who is richer or more successful.

21. The character realizes they are tired of pretending to be less intelligent, more conventional, or more reserved than they actually are in order to be acceptable to the partner. Maybe a friend or family member points out this dynamic.

22. The character strongly prefers a different physical appearance or body type, or learns that their partner strongly prefers a physical appearance or body type that's very different from their own. Maybe their partner's words about it on a certain occasion are the breaking point.

23. The character is starting a new school or a job in a new city and doesn't want to try a long-distance relationship; they would prefer a fresh start.

24. The character feels that their partner now takes them for granted, no longer showing appreciation or making efforts to be romantic.

25. The character falls for someone else.

50 PLOT TWISTS

Unexpected turns and dramatic reveals are one of the great pleasures of novels and movies. They're the reason why many people hate spoilers. A well-executed plot twist can keep readers riveted. When they didn't know it was coming but then look back and realize there were hints all along, it's really satisfying.

1. Someone who was presumed dead is still alive. In a supernatural or speculative story, he may have actually died and been resurrected.

2. Variation of the above: the ghost haunting them is actually someone who's still alive and pretending to be a ghost.

3. A character turns out to be a ghost.

4. A character turns out to be a delusion—or another identity of a character who has dissociative identity disorder.

5. The character has only been pretending to have a grandma, a significant other, or a child.

6. She's not a mom. She's been referring to her pets as "her children" or "her babies," and they have very human-sounding names.

7. The character has a secret spouse or a secret child.

8. A character has been pretending to be someone else.

9. A character has been faking an illness, a disability, or a mental disorder.

10. The grave or crypt holds the remains of a different person.

11. A character has been living in the attic or basement of the house, or on the grounds.

12. A character unexpectedly seduces someone.

13. Two characters have been romantically involved all along.

14. Someone has a twin or a clone.

15. Two characters are revealed to be siblings, or parent and child.

16. Someone suddenly remembers his true identity.

17. Everyone finds out that a character has been possessed or controlled by some other person or entity.

18. A seemingly average and ordinary character reveals himself to be a genius, fabulously rich, or in possession of remarkable skills.

19. The supposed billionaire or heiress has run out of money.

20. A love interest turns out to be the son or daughter of a boss, coworker, or enemy.

21. The person who thinks they are the grifter is actually being grifted.

22. The outlandish thing an eccentric person kept insisting was real? It's real.

23. The problem is revealed to be just part of a much bigger and more horrible problem.

24. Some small concern or aberration that nobody paid much attention to turns out to be the biggest problem of all.

25. Someone's attempt to solve a problem makes it ten times worse.

26. Someone's efforts to prevent something awful actually makes it happen.

27. They were much closer to salvation—the shore, the surface, or so on—than they realized.

28. A character faces a difficult moral choice—and decides to do the wrong thing.

29. The dreaded event comes to pass—but it turns out to be a good thing.

30. A wish comes true—with disastrous consequences.

31. A victory is so costly that it eventually sets someone up for a final defeat.

32. Each character has double-crossed the other.

33. Someone who was acting like an enemy reveals herself as an ally.

34. A trusted ally turns out to be an enemy.

35. The parent arranged the kidnapping.

36. The victim arranged their own kidnapping.

37. The sorority house, yoga retreat, or rehab center turns out to be a cult compound.

38. The outside world or their home planet was not, as they believed, turned into an unlivable dystopia.

39. The character is actually working for an evil boss or company—or one with a big secret.

40. The character has been tricked into being the accessory to a crime.

41. The character knew they were being conned, but thought they had the con figured out. They were wrong.

42. A military drill is actually real.

43. A supposed novel is actually nonfiction.

44. Their dream life is actually their real life.

45. An elaborate setting, such as a corporate office, a government facility, or a nightclub, is fake.

46. The destroyed object or artifact was a fake.

47. The replica was actually the original.

48. An imaginary person that the character invented shows up.

49. They've killed or imprisoned an innocent person.

50. They've helped the wrong person escape.

50 FUNNY PLOT POINTS

It's all in the way you handle it, of course, but here are fifty situations that could lend themselves to a hilarious scene.

1. They're pretending to be someone they're not, but they don't look the part and/or have the required knowledge.

2. They don't realize right away that they've been mistaken for somebody else.

3. They have no idea who they're with, and as a result, they do something wildly inappropriate.

4. They walk in on a situation they *really* didn't expect.

5. They break into the wrong hotel room or house.

6. Someone attempts to rescue a person who doesn't need rescuing.

7. An apparently mild-mannered or harmless-looking person turns out to be the wrong person to mess with.

8. It turns out that someone has a surprising hobby, or is a fan of something totally unexpected.

9. It turns out that someone has a surprising alter ego.

10. Someone tries to please two or more characters with very different demands simultaneously.

11. Someone is making the barest minimum effort at a task or job.

12. They're trying to hide something that's very difficult to hide.

13. Their friend, family member, or pet completely embarrasses them with inappropriate behavior.

14. One person thought this would be a fun date or party idea. It isn't.

15. They take someone's words way too literally and act accordingly.

16. They accidentally attend the wrong wedding or funeral.

17. They're trying to carry themselves with dignity in a truly undignified situation.

18. They address a minor situation with over-the-top behavior.

19. They mess up a villain's furniture, desk at work, garden, or vehicle, pretending that it's an accident.

20. A seemingly tough character is revealed as being extremely shy.

21. A tough character completely melts in the presence of a cute animal.

22. A character is out of their comfort zone when dealing with a baby, child, or animal.

23. They're out of their comfort zone when doing something in front of a large audience.

24. They're out of their comfort zone because ordinarily, they would never go to this place or take part in this event.

25. They're forced to borrow clothes that don't suit them at all.

26. They are incredibly inappropriately dressed for the occasion.

27. They have a wardrobe malfunction.

28. They make others uncomfortable with their complete lack of modesty.

29. As a couple, they always overdo it with their public displays of affection.

30. The optimist and the pessimist have to work together.

31. The rule-follower and the rogue have to work together.

32. A character deliberately attempts to be unattractive or unappealing to another character.

33. A silly challenge or rivalry leads to petty, devious, or over-the-top measures.

34. A character doing something ridiculous is seen by someone they hoped to impress.

35. Someone is excited about something that everyone else finds mundane or boring.

36. Someone appears unimpressed by a truly wonderful turn of events.

37. One character is not at all in a hurry; the other one definitely is.

38. A character is trying to leave, but different people keep delaying them.

39. A character discovers that this first date was a disastrous idea.

40. A sophisticated snob attends a low-class event.

41. A crass person attends a very sophisticated event.

42. A person who's clearly ill pretends they're completely fine.

43. Characters put on a very bad performance or create a very bad video or commercial.

44. One character cannot understand why everyone else is so enthusiastic about a certain person, activity, or event.

45. A character hides from someone who's being annoying, whiny, or demanding.

46. One person is thrilled about a turn of events that nobody else is happy about.

47. A character becomes much less restrained while under the influence of alcohol, medication, or a magical spell.

48. Someone believes they're interviewing for a very different kind of job than the one they're actually interviewing for.

49. They say yes to an invitation—and then realize what they've actually agreed to.

50. They pretend to detest something they actually enjoy.

50 PLOT POINTS TO BREAK READERS' HEARTS

Not every story is happy, and even stories with happy endings may have some heartbreak on the way there. These plot points will make readers feel for your characters—and keep them reading, in hopes that everything turns out all right in the end.

If you are looking for plot points that are even more tragic, you can find some in my list of past traumas.

1. a child gets picked last for a team

2. none of the invited guests show up for the party

3. a much-anticipated holiday gathering or big event is ruined by a fight or bad behavior

4. a character is excited about giving a gift—and the other person hates it

5. a character can't afford to buy a gift for a loved one

6. someone belatedly receives a letter, gift, or drawing from someone who has since passed away

7. a character has no one to spend the holidays with

8. someone at a craft fair or farmers market is unable to sell anything

9. a gambler loses big

10. a person's life savings are wiped out due to exorbitant medical costs, a financial crash, or a scam

11. someone loses something of great financial and/or sentimental value

12. a character has a breakdown after a terrible day at work

13. a good candidate loses the election

14. a character's well-meaning advice causes harm to someone they love

15. a formerly competent, stable person is now living an impoverished or dangerous life due to addiction

16. someone learns about their shocking family history

17. someone learns that their idol is not a good person

18. someone's significant other breaks up with them

19. someone tells a character they can no longer be friends

20. someone's ex-partner or unrequited crush gets married to somebody else

21. someone gets up the courage to say "I love you" to the person they're dating, and that person doesn't say it back

22. someone tells their long-time partner, "I don't love you"

23. a child tells their doting parent, "I don't love you"

24. a character thinks of ending their life due to physical pain

25. a character finds out their loved one is thinking of ending their life

26. a character loses their scholarship due to low grades or a bad decision

27. someone doesn't make the team or the cast of the play

28. someone doesn't get the job after multiple interviews

29. a character's new boss makes a move on them

30. someone overhears someone they trust speaking badly of them

31. someone is the victim of racial profiling

32. someone who ran away from their abusive spouse, parent, or cult leader is returned to them

33. a character is told they will never succeed or never be good enough

34. someone gives up on a dream they pursued for years

35. a character who's had a rough life speaks of their lifetime dream— and it's so modest, it's heartbreaking

36. the team doesn't win the big game

37. a family member isn't invited to a birthday, graduation, or wedding

38. a parent doesn't show up for a child's birthday, graduation, or wedding

39. a child seeks out their birth parent, who wants nothing to do with them

40. a parent who made mistakes tries to have a relationship with their adult child, but their child wants nothing to do with them

41. someone is stood up for a lunch or a date they were looking forward to

42. someone proposes marriage and is rejected

43. friends or a dating couple have to part ways

44. a pet is injured or becomes ill

45. a pet is lost or abandoned

46. an adult child has to tell their parent that they need to go into assisted living

47. an aging romantic partner or family member can no longer remember the people in their life

48. a parent, grandparent, or trusted mentor dies

49. a parent has to tell a child about the death of a loved one

50. a child not old enough to understand death wants their dead loved one to come back, or wake up

50 PLOT POINTS FOR WISH FULFILLMENT

Many readers *love* stories that allow them to feel what it would be like to have their wishes come true. It can make people feel more hopeful and positive about their real lives. Some of the things on this list are major, and some are smaller victories, but they all have the potential for a satisfying plot point. Many of them could be happy endings.

1. becoming rich after a long period of poverty

2. becoming famous after a long period of toiling in obscurity

3. finally being recognized as the person who accomplished something important, after someone else hid this fact or took credit for it

4. saving another person, or a lot of them, from death

5. making a great escape from a deadly situation

6. having your abuser or oppressor arrested

7. being able to snub a person who snubbed you in the past

8. being able to fire someone who used to bully you at the workplace

9. transforming yourself into a stronger, more beautiful, or more stylish person

10. being desired by a wildly desirable person

11. being desired by many people, and having your choice of dates

12. having many friends after being an outcast

---

13. performing or speaking in public successfully after being too scared to do so

14. "going viral" or having your fifteen minutes of fame for a positive reason

15. being reunited with a loved one

16. having a baby after struggles with fertility

17. finding a lost pet

18. traveling to a beautiful place—or traveling around the world

19. traveling to a magical or alien world

20. traveling to another time period

21. destroying a cursed object

22. walking out on a toxic partner

23. walking out on a toxic job

24. burning an evil place to the ground

25. making others realize that they've grossly underestimated you

26. as the underdog, winning the whole thing

27. making an amazing scientific breakthrough

28. discovering one has a supernatural power

29. being smart enough to solve a complex puzzle or win at a difficult game

30. being a better fighter than anyone else

31. being faster than anyone else

32. creating a masterpiece, such as a painting, book, sculpture, song, or movie

33. pulling off a daring heist

34. having a fairy godmother, guardian angel, pet dragon, or some other powerful fantasy friend

35. being cured of a disease or disability

36. a loved one who seemed likely to die making a full recovery

37. a community setting differences aside for a common mission

38. being forgiven for a big transgression

39. getting a second chance at love with the "one who got away"

40. being elected as a world leader

41. finding out that one is actually royalty

42. being found by a kind parent or guardian after being an orphan or being raised by cruel parents

43. getting a chance to live life, or part of it, over again

44. being energetic, joyful, and/or heroic in your old age

45. finding romantic love late in life

46. finding out that a loved one, believed to be dead, is still alive

47. having a loved one come back from the dead

48. going to heaven or a better place

49. outwitting a villain or defeating them in battle

50. being the only one who can save the world

3. SETTING

For many writers, setting can be an afterthought. In fact, it's a powerful secret weapon. A evocative setting can help readers feel swept away into the world of the story. It can underscore the mood of the scene, or provide an ironic contrast—a couple having a bitter argument in Disneyland, for example. A setting can pose a unique challenge in an action scene, amplify the sweep of a romantic scene, or even provide the central conflict.

Some writers imagine that to establish a setting, they will have to write long paragraphs of description, but this isn't true. The details can be shared here and there. For instance, if two people are talking and hiking in the Arizona desert, at different points in the scene, we can mention the fuzzy teddy bear cholla, the blue mountains in the distance, or the smell of the creosote bushes after the rain.

It's a good idea to evoke a sense of place near the beginning of a scene, and especially near the beginning of the novel—unless ambiguity about the setting serves the story.

A few years back on social media, I asked writers what settings they wanted cheat sheets for. The lists of details in this section are based partly on that feedback. It's easy for writers to forget to use sound and scent when setting a scene, but appealing to other senses in addition to sight will make your book more accessible to everyone and more immersive.

100 CONTEMPORARY
SETTINGS FOR SCENES

If you're in the middle of writing a novel or script, and you're getting a little bored, maybe you and your characters could use a change of scenery. It's natural to have many scenes set at the character's home, their place of work, or their school, but putting them in another place might give you a fresh perspective—or even a breakthrough in your story.

Some of these might be good locations for a meet cute in a romance novel—or a murder in a mystery novel. You can also use this list for simple writing prompts.

1. airplane
2. airport
3. train
4. train station
5. bus
6. rowboat
7. cruise ship
8. park
9. dog park
10. movie theater
11. laundromat
12. barber shop
13. beauty salon
14. nail salon
15. spa
16. swimming pool
17. beach
18. hot tub
19. ski slope
20. ice skating rink
21. hotel lobby
22. hotel room
23. homeless shelter
24. tent
25. hiking trail
26. church, temple, or mosque
27. bridge
28. balcony
29. rooftop
30. backyard
31. coffee shop

32. bookstore

33. library

34. funeral home

35. cemetery

36. old-fashioned video arcade

37. pizzeria

38. ice cream parlor

39. school

40. football stadium

41. ball park

42. golf course or mini golf course

43. basketball, tennis, or pickleball court

44. post office

45. parking lot

46. car dealership

47. gas station

48. highway

49. police station

50. bakery

51. diner

52. fast-food restaurant

53. fine dining restaurant

54. drugstore

56. waiting room at doctor's office or hospital

57. emergency room

58. veterinary clinic

59. grocery store

60. farmers market

61. plant nursery/ garden center

62. home improvement store

63. "big box" discount store

64. bank of a lake or river

65. apple orchard

66. cornfield

67. barn

68. thrift shop

69. estate sale

70. real estate open house

71. construction site

72. opera house

73. music festival

74. Renaissance fair

75. theme park

76. state fair

77. Pride parade

78. fireworks show

79. Christmas tree lighting ceremony

80. children's recital

81. bridal boutique

82. dry cleaner's

83. winery or brewery

84. nightclub

85. sports bar

86. liquor store

87. vape shop

88. gun range

89. tattoo parlor

90. alley

91. public restroom

92. fitting room in
a clothing store or
department store

93. gym/fitness center

94. assisted living
community

95. art museum/gallery

96. planetarium

97. bike shop

98. courtroom

99. abandoned factory

100. secret bunker

WAYS TO DESCRIBE WEATHER

Many writing instructors and editors will tell you not to open a novel with a description of the weather. However, several great novels do exactly that, which just goes to show that no writing advice applies to every story. Weather can make a setting feel more real, underscore the mood of a scene, provide an ironic contrast, or serve as an obstacle or a catalyst.

HOT WEATHER

sun-soaked

sun-drenched

sun-blasted

blazing sunshine

fiery sun

fierce sun

glaring sun

white-hot sun

baking in the sun

scorching heat

extravagant heat

relentless sun

heavy air

muggy air

dank air

like a sauna

steamy

sticky

dense heat

tropical heat

sultry

dusty heat

arid heat

like an oven

like a furnace

like a kiln

heat beating down

heat rising from the earth

withering heat

radiating heat

blistering heat

oppressive heat

miserable heat

insufferable heat

stifling heat

suffocating heat

stultifying heat

heat pressing down

heat permeating
one's clothes

heat making one sleepy

heat seeping into one's skin

searing sun

shimmering heat

waves of heat rising

horizon wobbling
in the heat

WARM WEATHER

a beautiful day

a fine day

a clear day

a mild day

a temperate day

a golden day

a glorious day

heavenly weather

bright and sunny

a gorgeous spring day

a dazzling summer day

a brilliant autumn day

a vivid blue sky

a cloudless sky

fluffy white clouds

cotton ball clouds

cotton candy clouds

gentle sunshine

lazy sunshine

kind sunshine

filtered sunlight

dappled sunlight

welcome warmth

one of those rare days

a day that made one
forget one's worries

COOL WEATHER

crisp, clear air

air crisp as an apple

fresh, clean air

stimulating air

invigorating air

bracing air

a nip in the air

a brisk day

a chilly day

weak sunshine

clammy air

damp air

GRAY, OVERCAST SKIES

gloomy sky

dreary day

a misty day

cozy gray day

a soft gray sky

sky like gray wool

a dove-gray sky

colorless sky

sunless sky

steel-gray sky

leaden sky

stony sky

granite sky

cement-gray sky

ominous gray sky

threatening clouds

foreboding clouds

COLD WEATHER

frosty air

icy air

Arctic air

glacial air

bitter cold

brutal cold

cruel cold

bone-chilling cold

bone-cracking cold

penetrating cold

numbing cold

punishing cold

dangerous cold

unforgiving cold

too cold to talk

cold knifing through
one's clothes

cold burning one's lungs

cold taking one's
breath away

WIND

an icy blast

a gust of wind

wild wind

raw wind

stiff wind

insistent winds

heavy winds

strong winds

cutting wind

whipping winds

biting wind

harsh wind

angry wind

wintry squall

violent gale

howling wind

shifting winds

restless wind

blustery

fresh breeze

soft breeze

balmy breeze

perfumed breeze

breeze like a caress

slight breeze

hint of a breeze

stirring breeze

breeze lifting one's hair

wind whipping one's hair

wind rustling through trees

like a warm breath

hot wind

desert wind

dry wind

like a blast from
a hair dryer

RAIN

a fine drizzle

gray drizzle

spitting rain

stinging rain

steady rain

rain falling in torrents

pebbles of falling rain

shower of rain

a veil of rain

a curtain of rain

sheets of rain

cascades of rain

squall of rain

deluge

downpour

rain beating down

hard-driving rain

pelting rain

lashing rain

slashing rain

pattering rain

rain spattering the sidewalk

rain speckling the
windshield

rain hammering the roof

rain pounding the patio

rain glossing the streets

rain dampening one's face

bowing one's head
against the rain

squinting against the rain

THUNDER AND LIGHTNING

rumbling in the distance

a roll of distant thunder

growl of thunder

crash of thunder

crackle of thunder

crack of thunder

clap of thunder

bang of thunder

booming thunder

rattled with thunder

earth-shaking thunder

tempestuous

a furious storm

flash of lightning

flashes of lightning
like a strobe

streaks of lightning

lightning slashing
through the sky

lighting slicing the sky

lightning branching
across the sky

a vein of lightning

a storm like hell unleashed

SNOW AND ICE

flurries of snow

dancing flakes

snowflakes floating down

snowflakes wafting down

snowflakes stinging
one's face

swirling snow

falling thick and fast

snow falling like ash

snow falling like confetti

big flakes falling like petals

flakes drifting down
like feathers

snow crunching underfoot

blinding snowstorm

snowbound

raging blizzard

glistening snow

sparkling expanses

blankets of white

carpet of snow

dollops of snow

caked with snow

snow like frosting
on a cake

boulders of snow

mounds of snow

snow-clad pines

branches furred with snow

snow sliding/
blowing off trees

branches coated in ice

roads/sidewalks
glazed with ice

glittering ice

icicles like teeth

icicles like stalactites

spears of ice

daggers of ice

shards of ice

frost patterns like lace

frost patterns like ferns

crystallized by frost

silvered with frost

FOG

clouds of mist

dense fog

swirling mist

billowing fog

cloaked in mist

cocooned in fog

shrouded in fog

enveloped by fog

smothered by fog

made mysterious by fog

the fog rolled in

the fog was burning off

the fog was lifting

the fog was clearing

the fog was dissipating

LIST OF SCENTS

The sense of smell is uniquely connected to memories and to emotion. A scent in a story can flip a little switch in a reader's brain, immediately triggering nostalgia, comfort, fear, or disgust. A character's scent, or the scent of their home or their car, can reveal something about them. A certain smell can be a clue in a mystery, or an element of attraction in a romance. And it can make readers feel like they're *in* the story.

With this list, I didn't try to list every food and every plant there is. I focused on the more common ones in the U.S. There are a few smells on here that are almost extinct, so you might not be personally familiar with them. Some of these scents come in a lot of different varieties.

aftershave

algae

almonds

ammonia

apples

asphalt (blacktop)

babies/the top of a baby's head

baby powder

bacon

bad breath/halitosis

ballpoint pen ink

bananas

Band-Aids

Barbicide

basil

basketball, especially new

beer

birthday cake

birthday candles, just blown out

bleach

blood (regular blood; period blood)

body odors

books, old

bread, fresh-baked

burned match

burning leaves

buttercream frosting

calamine lotion

cannabis

cardamom

carnations

car exhaust

car interior, new

carpet (new; dirty)

cat litter box

cedar/cedar chests

celery

charcoal briquettes

chewing gum

chocolates

cigar smoke

cigarette smoke

cilantro

cinnamon

cinnamon rolls

citronella

clay

clover

cloves

coconut

coffee

cookies

crayons

creosote bushes

cucumbers

curry

decomposing body

deodorant

dill

diesel fumes

dirt

dirty diapers

dog, unwashed or wet

dog's paws (like corn chips)

donuts

dusty light bulb

clothes dryer sheets

dryer vents

dumpster/garbage

Durian fruit

eucalyptus

excrement (human, dog, horse, manure)

fallen leaves (dry, wet)

figs

fireworks, burned

frankincense

French fries

fried chicken

garlic

gasoline

glue

grapefruit

graphite (pencil lead)

grass, freshly mowed

hand sanitizer
(ethyl alcohol)

hair (washed, oily, burned)

hairspray

honeysuckle

incense

infected wound

jasmine

Kool-Aid

lava (includes smell
of sulfur)

lavender

laundry detergent

laundry, fresh or dirty

leather

lemon

lemon furniture polish

lighter fluid

lilacs

lilies

lime

linseed oil

lumber

Lysol

magnolias

markers

mascara

mayonnaise

mildew

mimeographed handouts

mineral spirits

mint

Miracle-Gro

mothballs

musk

musty basement

nail polish

nail polish remover

natural gas/gas leak

new clothes in a store

Noxema/cold cream

onions

oranges/orange juice

orange blossoms

oregano

ozone (approaching storm)

PVC vinyl (shower
curtain; beach ball)

paint (oil paint, house
paint, spray paint)

pancakes with maple syrup

patchouli

peaches

peanut butter

pears

peonies

perfume (countless
varieties)

perm solution for hair

petrichor: the smell
when it rains

pie (lots of different kinds)

pine trees

Pine-Sol floor cleaner

pineapple

pizza

Play-Doh

popcorn

pumpkin spice lattes

rice, cooked

rosemary

rotten food (eggs, fish,
meat, potatoes)

rotting wood

rubber cement

rubbing alcohol

roses

saddle soap

sage

sandalwood

sawdust

school paste

Scotch tape

scented candles
(countless varieties)

the sea/sea spray

shampoo

shaving cream

shoes (new shoes;
stinky sneakers)

shoe polish

soap

skunk

spoiled milk

steak

strawberries

sweat

sweet grass

swimming pools
with chlorine

suntan lotion

tar

tea

tea tree oil

tennis balls in a
just-opened can

Thanksgiving turkey

tires, especially new

tomatoes/tomato vines

tuna salad

unwashed socks

unwashed underwear

urine

vanilla

varnish

Vicks VapoRub

vinegar

vintage vinyl records

vomit

WD-40

waffle cone

wallpaper paste

watermelon

whiskey

Windex/glass cleaner

wine

winter air on someone's coat/skin

wood smoke

wood wax

wool (including wet winter coats)

yeast

ylang-ylang

DETAILS FOR A CREEPY SETTING

Many of these things aren't *always* creepy! It depends on the context. And of course, a talented horror or suspense writer can make us see ordinary objects and situations in a new, creepy light.

SIGHTS

storm clouds

swirling dead leaves

bare branches

a full moon

owls

vultures

crows

scarecrows

long shadows

dark roads

spiders

spiderwebs

rats

worms

lots of insects

dripping blood

peeling paint

broken windows

androids

old dolls

dollhouses

tattered stuffed animals

disturbing children's drawings

skeletons

skulls

masks

flickering light bulbs

flashing lightning

gravestones

hangman's noose

abandoned hospital room

abandoned prison cell

specimens in jars

handprints

footprints

eyes glowing red

eyes glowing in the dark

face or figure in mirror

certain clowns

complete darkness

claustrophobic spaces

surgical instruments

a barber's razor

manacles

bats

snakes

Ouija boards

funhouse mirrors

poppets/voodoo dolls

Ten of Swords Tarot card

Devil Tarot card

Death Tarot card

glitching TV or video

duct tape in
unexpected place

fallen trees

cabinet doors all
standing open

tooth, animal or human

taxidermized animals

marionettes

portraits of dour-
looking people

mannequins

fire damage

windows that can't
be opened

doors with broken locks

red curtains, carpet,
and walls

furniture with claw feet

SOUNDS

branches creaking
in the wind

playground swings creaking

thunder

flapping wings

buzzing bees or flies

creaking doors

creaking stairs

footsteps

music box

ticking clock

crackling vinyl records

radio or TV static

chainsaw

dentist's drill

unhinged laughter

child's laughter

child singing

talking toys

talking pet birds

AI voices

scraping at the window

banging at the door

someone turning
the doorknob

growls

whispers

screams

moans

dripping water

heartbeat

a notification on a
phone or computer

silence

SMELLS

musty odors

decaying odors

DETAILS FOR A CHRISTMAS SETTING

Many of these may be specific to the U.S., or to cultures or regions within the U.S.

SIGHTS

Santa Claus

Mrs. Claus

Santa's bag full of toys

elves

reindeer

sleighs

angels

toy soldiers

inflatable yard decorations

decorative figurines

Christmas village sets

luminaria

twinkling lights

extremely decorated houses

Nativity scenes

paper snowflakes

falling snow

snow on trees, rooftops, cars

snowmen

icicles

cardinals

pinecones

poinsettias: red, white, pink

holly

hanging mistletoe

Christmas cards on the mantel

wrapped gifts

ribbons and bows

pine trees

decorated Christmas trees

shiny glass ornaments

tinsel and tinsel garlands

popcorn and cranberry garland

evergreen garlands

star or angel tree topper

crowded parking lots

crowded shops

elaborate store
window displays

candles

candy canes

gingerbread people

gingerbread houses

ice skates

ice skating rink or pond

sleds

Santa hats

winter scarves

mittens

"ugly" sweaters

toy train sets

wreaths on doors,
windows, cars

stockings hung
on the mantel

family group photos
for cards

festive matching pajamas

wooden nutcrackers

North Pole, depicted
as actual pole

Santa's toy workshop

snow globes

Elf on a Shelf

parades

decorated sugar cookies

red and/or green quilts

mailboxes full of cards

Advent wreaths
with candles

Advent calendars

churches

skyscrapers lit with
holiday designs

wish lists

shopping bags from stores

packages at the door

red potted amaryllis

SOUNDS

sleigh bells—on reindeer,
horses, or doors

reindeer hooves
on the rooftop

feet crunching in snow

shoveling snow or
snow blower

snowplows clearing
the roads

Christmas carols

Tchaikovsky's *The
Nutcracker Suite*

"Hallelujah Chorus" from
Handel's *Messiah*

church organ

church bells

tearing wrapping paper

loud toys on Christmas morning

crackling fire

SMELLS

evergreen trees

cinnamon

mulling spices

bayberry candles

fire in the fireplace

wet wool coats

baking and cooking smells (see below)

TASTES

Favorites vary from community to community, and from family to family, but here are some popular ones.

hot chocolate

eggnog

peppermint mocha

mulled wine

gingerbread

spritz cookies

shortbread cookies

roasted turkey

baked ham

prime rib

sage stuffing

cornbread dressing

sweet potato casserole

green bean casserole

lasagna

macaroni and cheese

peppermint bark

fruitcake

red velvet cake

cinnamon buns

mince pies

fudge

candy canes

nuts, with a nutcracker

sweet potato pies

the Feast of the Seven Fishes

tamales eaten on Christmas Eve

arroz con gandules

coquitos

stollen

pierogis

DETAILS FOR AN OFFICE SETTING

SIGHTS

trash receptacles outside the entrance to the building

sign with company name and/or logo in lobby

ID card reader

rows of beige cubicles

framed family photos in cubicles and offices

sticky notes on computer monitors

rows of desks and computers in an open seating area

gray or beige carpet, subtle stripe or geometrical pattern

white ceiling tiles

light fixtures flush with ceiling

exit signs

beige or black steel filing cabinets

beige steel supply cabinet

metal file organizers on desktops

pens and markers in holders

white dry-erase boards

motivational posters

posters about employee law and/or office safety

fire extinguisher under glass

desk chairs on wheels

conference rooms and/or offices with one glass wall

fake wood conference tables

fake wood and/or steel desks

big windows with blinds

mugs with random sayings in kitchen/break room

boxes of photocopier paper

flattened corrugate
shipping boxes in or
near recycling bin

clear plastic mats under
desk chairs on wheels

wall calendars depicting
dogs, cats, or travel
destinations, in
cubicles and offices

printer and photocopy
machines

bulletin boards

pushpins

flipcharts on easels

indoor bins for trash
and recycling

tape dispensers

headphones

window washers suspended
on the outside of a
high-rise building

plaques and trophies—
industry awards
and recognition

user manuals

three-ring binders

wall clocks

ID badges on lanyards

black leather chairs in
executive offices and
executive conference rooms

large screens in executive
conference rooms

communal refrigerator

blankets or sweaters
draped over office
chairs in cold offices

personal fans in cubicles
in hot offices

planners

large purses, backpacks, or
messenger bags in cubicles

pads of lined paper—white,
or yellow legal pads

index cards

piles of reports and meeting
handouts on a desk

coats hanging from
plastic hooks

snacks in drawers

wire letter trays

water coolers with
paper cups

indoor plants

potted trees, real or fake

name plates on desks, or
outside cubicles or offices

boxes and padded
envelopes for shipping

bowls of candy for visitors
on reception desks

business cards

white takeout boxes of
Chinese food or empty
pizza boxes, if people
have been working late

yellow plastic easels on
floors reading "Caution:
Slippery When Wet"

SOUNDS

elevator doors opening
and closing

'ding' when elevators
doors open

hum of air conditioner
or heating

buzz of fluorescent lights

computers starting
up or rebooting

tapping of fingers on
computer keyboards; click
of computer mouse

clicking notification for Slack

chiming notification for a
new email or an upcoming
meeting on the calendar

tapping pen on desk

clicking pen

marker squeaking on
flipchart or dry erase board

telephones ringing

automated voicemail voice

cell phones vibrating
or pinging

photocopy machine:
beeping buttons, paper
shuffling sounds

microwave: beeps,
whirring sounds

ka-chunk of stapler

vending machine: beeping
buttons, whine of
machine grabbing drink
or snack; coins falling

soda can being opened

whine of paper shredder

whispering

sniffling

blowing nose

coughing

sneezing

chatter

laughter

fire alarm

SMELLS

car exhaust in parking garage

coffee

coworker's cologne
or perfume

burned microwave popcorn

rotten food in
communal fridge

Sharpie markers

TASTES

bagels, donuts (for a
meeting, or because
it's Friday)

coffee

soft drinks

chips and candy from
the vending machine

DETAILS FOR A HOSPITAL SETTING

SIGHTS

surgeons in scrubs, often teal or green

doctors and nurses in scrubs, often blue

surgical scrub caps, often light blue fabric or disposable blue polypropylene

surgical masks, often blue or white

hospital gowns, often blue or blue-and-white print

employees wearing ID badges on lanyards

wall-mounted hand sanitizer dispensers near entrances and elevators

connected rows of chairs in waiting room

stacks of magazines on tables in waiting room

vending machines for soft drinks, coffee, and snacks

patient registration kiosks, with employees behind glass partitions

vinyl floors

white acoustic tile on ceilings

wayfinding signs on walls and above hallways: arrows to maternity ward, radiology

TVs in waiting rooms and patient rooms

LED screens on stands or walls with health information and advertisements for pharmaceuticals

posters with health information and advertisements for pharmaceuticals

framed artwork in hallways, often abstract or scenic

colorful murals in children's hospitals or pediatric wards

beds with railings on the sides, adjustable for lying flat or sitting up

gurneys

wheelchairs

walkers

I.V. poles with plastic bags of fluids

monitors, often on rolling stands, tracking patients' vital signs such as cardiac activity (EKG), oxygen saturation, blood pressure, and temperature

defibrillators

wall-mounted holder for boxes of disposable blue nitrile gloves

red emergency phones near patient rooms and elevators, connected to the nurses' station

red outlets in operating rooms, hooked up to generators in case of power outages

screens for laparoscopic surgeries suspended from operating room ceiling

large lights suspended from operating room ceiling

supply cabinets for surgical and other medical supplies

chapels

cafeterias

coffee shops, sometimes affiliated with a national chain

in some hospitals: statues of Jesus, the Virgin Mary, or saints

in some hospitals: crosses

gift shops

bouquets of flowers

balloons with get-well messages

stuffed animals, as get-well gifts

SOUNDS

beeping heart monitors

buzz of fluorescent lights

crinkling paper spread on an exam table

the sound of a room divider curtain being pulled back

talking

shouting

groaning

snoring

babies and children crying

adults crying

music playing in an operating room—usually rock or classical

SMELLS

disinfectants

bleach-based cleaning products in restrooms

hand sanitizer

rubbing alcohol wipes

adhesive bandages

feces

urine

vomit

blood (a coppery smell)

fried food from the cafeteria

coffee

DETAILS FOR A U.S. CITY SETTING

SIGHTS

high-rise buildings
of glass and steel

brick apartment buildings

independent shops and
small businesses

unique restaurants
serving many different
kinds of cuisine

art galleries and museums

flyers on light poles about
politics, rock shows,
and missing pets

fire escapes

dogs or cats sitting
in windows

orange construction
cones and barriers

green street signs

traffic lights

streetlamps

banners hanging
from streetlamps,
advertising festivals,
museum exhibitions, or
neighborhood pride

cars

buses

trains

subway stations

bridges

pigeons

office workers

tourists with backpacks

shoppers with bags

doormen in front of
apartments and hotels

people sitting on front
steps of houses and
apartment buildings

bicyclists

people riding scooters

skyscrapers

clouds reflected in the
windows of tall buildings

churches, temples,
and mosques

produce and flower stands

carts selling pretzels, hot
dogs, gyros, and other foods

food trucks selling tacos,
falafel, ice cream, barbecue,
smoothies, gourmet
coffee drinks, and other
foods and drinks

fire hydrants

windows covered with
plywood on vacant buildings

vacant lots with litter

store windows with
retail displays

outdoor dining areas
at restaurants

trees growing in small plots
of earth along the sidewalks

rooftop gardens

street festivals, often
with music, food, or
heritage themes

steam rising from manholes
and orange and white striped
steam stacks (New York)

bags of trash piled on
sidewalks (New York)

dumpsters in alleys

parking garages with
signs for daily parking

large metal sculptures,
usually abstract

murals

graffiti on walls and
under bridges

people sitting on
sidewalks with signs
asking for donations

tent encampments of
unhoused people under
bridges and in other
areas (especially in cities
on the West Coast)

neon signs

billboards

sparkling city lights at night

wet streets and sidewalks
glistening at night

gray piles of snow

SOUNDS

cars whizzing by

cars honking

trucks beeping as
they back up

buses hissing as they stop

the screech of braking trains

recorded announcements,
on trains and subways

motorcycle engines

police, ambulance, and
fire engine sirens

tires splashing
through puddles

chatter of pedestrians

construction workers
shouting to one another

the whine and clang
of a garbage truck

the grinding and
brushing sounds of a
street sweeper truck

jackhammers

music played by street
musicians, including
drumming on five-
gallon buckets

deep bass thumping from
a car stereo speaker

music coming from open
doors of bars and clubs

church bells

SMELLS

car exhaust

diesel exhaust from buses

cigarette smoke

freshly baked cupcakes and/
or bread, from bakeries

freshly made donuts,
from donut shops

smells from other
restaurants: garlic, grilled
meat, and more

garbage

body odor, especially
in enclosed spaces

wet and/or hot asphalt

musty smell from
subway grates

urine

human feces

horse feces, in city parks
with horse-drawn carriages
or mounted police

dog feces

sulfur or rotten egg
smells near wastewater
treatment plants

yeasty, sour smells
near breweries

DETAILS FOR A U.S. SUBURBAN SETTING

Not surprisingly, this list overlaps both the urban and the small town lists.

SIGHTS

rows of identical or similar houses

in many newer homes: large kitchens, open floor plans, walk-in closets

attached garages; residents may usually enter the house from the garage

neatly mowed lawns

shrubs and garden beds in the front of houses

swimming pools

people walking their dogs

people pushing their babies and young children in strollers

children on bicycles, skateboards, and scooters

garages with so much stuff in them, the car is in the driveway

garage sales and yard sales

large bins of trash and recycling at the curbs

subdivision entrance signs (e.g. "Maple Hill," "Hawthorne Estates")

signs in front yards celebrating birthdays, graduations, or new births

basketball hoops in driveways

white picket fences (rare, but iconic symbol of suburbia)

tall white vinyl fences in backyards

kids selling lemonade or Girl Scout cookies at tables in front yards

UPS delivery trucks

giant grocery stores and
discount stores with
giant parking lots

strip malls with stores from
large corporate chains

restaurants from large
corporate chains

SOUNDS

lawn mowers

weed whackers

playing children—shouts
and laughter

barking dogs

bouncing basketballs

whacks of tennis
balls and pickleballs
from public courts

neighbors chatting

airplanes

distant highway traffic

raking

ice cream truck music

crickets

hammering, from new
construction or remodels

SMELLS

freshly cut grass

lilacs in spring (northeastern
and central U.S.)

neighbors grilling
meat outdoors

neighbors burning leaves

DETAILS FOR A U.S. SMALL TOWN SETTING

SIGHTS

water towers

a Main Street or town square lined with brick buildings

small businesses and local restaurants

diners, maybe named after the owner and/or featuring a decades-old sign

antique shops

quilt shops

VFW halls

vacant storefronts

one stoplight in the center of town

older homes

historic homes in disrepair

U.S. flags hanging from porches or near the front door

Christian churches topped with crosses or steeples

drivers and pedestrians waving at one another

drivers of two cars stopping in the street to have a conversation

small parades: one marching band, one float, cars and trucks

parks with gazebos

craft fairs—crafters selling their creations at tables

festivals, often with food or heritage themes

a packed high school football stadium on Friday night

closed shops and restaurants after six or seven p.m.

someone you know…
everywhere you go

SOUNDS

long conversations in
grocery checkout lines

the chugging and horns
of freight trains

the bells at railroad crossings

SMELLS

same as suburban and rural lists

DETAILS FOR A U.S. RURAL SETTING

SIGHTS

fields of hay, corn, soybeans, wheat, cotton, rice, sorghum, or sugar cane, depending on the region

orange groves or apple orchards, depending on the region

sunflower fields

uncultivated or fallow fields, sometimes covered with straw

creeks and ponds

pastures with grazing cattle or horses

feedlots

metal signs over private roads featuring the name of the ranch

wildflowers—varies by region, but may include dandelions, clover, violets, chicory, thistle, burdock, milkweed,

black-eyed Susans, goldenrod, oxeye daisies, bluebells, honeysuckle, or Queen Anne's lace

native grasses—varies by region, but may include bluestem varieties, Kentucky bluegrass, buffalo grass, foxtail, and switchgrass

bales of hay

older homes with large porches

big trees with tire swings

septic tanks outside houses

barns, red or weathered gray-brown wood

abandoned barns, sometimes collapsing

paintings on barns: American flags; square quilt designs; ads for local attractions; vintage ads for chewing tobacco, Coca-Cola, or Pepsi-Cola

steel grain elevators or silos

windpumps (metal windmills)

ATVs

tractors, including iconic green John Deere models

a slow tractor in front of you on the road

combines, seeders, and other farm equipment

split-rail fences

wire fences (barbed or smooth) with wooden posts

electric fences

old-fashioned metal mailboxes with flags, sometimes rusty

dirt roads

signs advertising country markets or fresh produce for sale at farms

signs advertising "U-Pick" berries, apples, or pumpkins

Christian billboards; anti-abortion billboards

pickup trucks, recent models and vintage

covered bridges (especially Pennsylvania, Ohio, Vermont, and Indiana)

a social gathering by a riverbank or large pond

deer

unobstructed views of rainbows, sunsets, and storm clouds rolling in

night skies filled with stars, thanks to lack of light pollution

SOUNDS

cows mooing

birds singing

rooster crowing

chickens squawking

horses neighing

cicadas and locusts buzzing

crickets chirping

owls hooting

SMELLS

newly mown hay

wet earth after rain

cow manure

DETAILS FOR A BEACH SETTING

SIGHTS

white-capped waves

white foam on the shore

footprints in the sand

messages written in the sand

sand dunes

blackened sand from
natural oil seeps

palm trees

seagrass waving in the wind

seagulls

other birds, such as pelicans,
sandpipers, and spoonbills

sunrises or sunsets
reflecting on the water

moonlight reflecting
on the water

wooden boardwalks

wooden piers

wooden lifeguard stands

large beach umbrellas

tents

lounge chairs

large, brightly patterned
beach towels

flip-flop sandals

sunglasses

coolers

large beach hats

plastic buckets and pails

beach balls

driftwood

seashells, especially in
the wet sand near the
shore at low tide

smooth stones—sometimes
stacked by beachgoers

sea glass

sea urchins, sea stars,
mussels, hermit crabs, and/
or small fish in tide pools

clumps of brown seaweed on the sand

large rocks at the shore, crusted with barnacles and shells

bonfires—or the charred remains of them

discarded bottles and cans

sailboats, motorboats, and yachts

buoys

oil tankers far offshore

children building sandcastles

people playing beach volleyball

people flying kites

dogs chasing balls and Frisbees

paddleboarders

kayakers

surfers

windsurfers

water-skiers

parasailers

jet skiers

hang gliders

people doing yoga

people posing for photos

joggers

sunbathers

bicyclists on beachfront sidewalks and trails

litter: empty plastic water bottles, bottle caps, cigarette butts, food wrappers, plastic garbage bags

long lines of cars on summer weekends to go to a big-city beach

portable toilets

cinderblock restrooms

murals for photo ops

turtles and turtle nests

scuba divers

faint phone screens— difficult to see in the bright sunlight

fallen coconuts

inner tubes

marina full of boats

hammocks

skateboarders at skateboard parks

roller skaters

street performers on
sidewalks and boardwalks

dolphins

whales

vendors selling artwork,
jewelry, or T-shirts

wedding and pregnancy
photo shoots

picnic tables

barbecue grills

dead sea slugs

SOUNDS

lapping or crashing waves

seagull cries

rock, rap, or other
music blasting from
portable speakers

laughter

children laughing,
shouting, squealing

SMELLS

sunscreen

suntan lotion
(coconut scent)

marijuana smoke,
in some states

TASTES

These are some foods frequently sold at stands and restaurants on boardwalks and near beaches in the U.S.

ice cream

frozen custard

tacos, especially fish tacos

corn dogs

hot dogs

pizza

French fries, straight
and curly

soft pretzels

popcorn—butter, cheese, caramel, or "kettle corn" seasoned with sugar and salt

poke bowls

acai bowls

crab cakes

lobster rolls (New England)

funnel cakes

saltwater taffy

fresh lemonade

margaritas

piña coladas

beer

DETAILS FOR A FOREST SETTING

Naturally, I'm not listing all the trees and plants in the U.S., but I'm including some of the most common ones.

SIGHTS

pines

firs

oaks

maples

ash trees

sweetgum trees

birches

dogwoods

alders

foliage

shade wildflowers, such as trillium (Midwestern and Eastern United States), lupines, violets, bluebells (Eastern North America), columbines, black cohosh, and jack in the pulpit

toadstools and mushrooms

lichen

ferns

cattails near bodies of water

wild blackberries and raspberries

wild leeks

wild ginger

moss—often on logs or rocks

sunlight filtering through trees

rough bark

smooth bark, like on birch and beech trees

carpets of dried leaves or pine needles

winding paths

trees casting long shadows

distant trees cloaked in mist

gnarled and twisted branches

the branches at the tops of
tall trees touching above you

bird nests

puddles

ravines

creeks

stone outcroppings

charred tree trunks
from a wildfire

the moon and/or lots of
bright stars above at night

thin branches of saplings
and shrubs blocking the path

spiderwebs…sometimes
beaded with rain

pine cones

acorns and acorn caps

buckeyes, from buckeye trees

spiky dried sweetgum fruits

fallen trees

butterflies

squirrels

chipmunks

deer—fawn, doe,
and/or buck

raccoons

rabbits

skunks

bears

animal tracks

human footprints

litter—discarded water
bottles, beer cans

snow-covered branches

frost

SOUNDS

chirping birds

trilling birds, such as
wood thrushes

warbling birds

chattering birds

tapping woodpeckers

hooting owls

screeching red-tailed hawks

cawing and croaking crows

flapping of bat wings

hum of june bug wings

buzz of mosquitos

chirping crickets

croaking frogs

coyote or wolf howl

squirrels running
across branches

wind rustling through
leaves and/or pine needles

babbling or rushing of a
nearby stream or creek

rumbling thunder

cracks of lightning

raindrops falling on leaves

footsteps

snapping of a twig
underfoot

squelching sound
of feet in mud

zipping/unzipping
of a tent flap

the hush of the
woods after snow

icicles dripping
during a thaw

SMELLS

rotting wood

decaying leaves

damp earth

fresh green leaves

sugary smell of maple
leaves in the fall

fresh pine needles
and pine resin

skunk

campfire smoke

DETAILS FOR A EUROPEAN MEDIEVAL CASTLE

SIGHTS

stone walls

whitewashed plaster walls

walls with painted murals or painted repeating motifs

candles in niches in the walls

bronze or iron candlesticks with prickets (spikes) to hold the candles

standing frames for embroidery projects

woven tapestries depicting saints, Biblical scenes, scenes from Roman mythology, or hunting scenes (12th century—onward)

rush mats (usually made of sweet flag plants) on floors

toilets—holes in a long wooden bench in a room called a garderobe

chamber pots, sometimes fitted into a wooden chair or cabinet

large wooden tub for bathing

combs of antler horn, bone, or ivory, sometimes elaborately carved (a popular gift from a lover to his lady)

trenchers—plates made of hollowed-out stale loaves of bread

white linen tablecloths

mazers—wooden drinking bowls, sometimes trimmed with silver

glazed earthenware pitchers and jugs, possibly decorated with motifs of animals, for milk, water, and wine

spoons—pewter, brass, or silver for nobility

glazed earthenware mugs

pewter or silver cups

flagons—large pitchers for
wine, water, or ale, made
from bronze, pewter, leather,
or glazed earthenware

pewter or earthenware dishes
for salt (shared at the table)

rats and mice

cats—as mousers, but
also as beloved pets

greyhounds and other hunting
dogs who lived indoors

big mastiffs as guard dogs

lapdogs, as pets for ladies

servant beds: straw
mattresses on the floor

beds for the nobility: wooden
posts and a wooden canopy,
possibly with elaborate carving

bed hangings: sometimes
brightly dyed; sometimes
elaborately embroidered;
sometimes tapestry
work featuring the
family coat of arms

woolen blankets

sunlight peeking through
small windows (no glass)

a Book of Hours—small
book of Christian prayers,
sometimes illuminated with
lavish designs; vellum pages
made from sheepskin or
calfskin, tooled leather cover

iron keys

pewter brooches used to
fasten cloaks—silver or
gold for the wealthy

elaborate rings of gold
and sapphire, ruby,
emerald, and/or pearl

small knives, often carried at
the belt, for eating and for
other uses; iron or steel

Anatolian rugs or "Turkish"
rugs, most often in geometric
and/or floral patterns, red
and gold often dominating
the color scheme (14th
century—onward)

iron nails for carpentry
and construction

carved oak or walnut chests
and cupboards (like modern
sideboards or buffets) for
dinnerware or for valuables

chairs with high backs, made of oak, ash, walnut, elm, or poplar, sometimes carved, gilded, and/or painted red or green, for the nobility

wooden benches for dining (much more common than individual chairs)

oak trestle tables

oak coffers with iron bands (large boxes with locks for storing valuables)

folding stools with leather seats

fireplaces—with chimneys, beginning in the 12th century

built-in stone, clay, or tiled ovens

iron cauldrons for cooking stew

butteries—cellar rooms for storing ale, wine, and possibly mead or liquor (aqua vitae)

pantries—rooms for storing and slicing bread

larders—cellar rooms for storing meats preserved in barrels of lard; cheese; and hanging rabbits, fowl, and fish

dovecotes—cylindrical buildings to house doves or pigeons, kept for meat, eggs, and fertilizer

icons—wooden panels, painted or carved, depicting saints

artwork depicting unicorns, associated with Jesus Christ

golden crowns encrusted with diamonds, rubies, emeralds, pearls, sapphires, and/or enamel

small pots of bronze or clay with pastes or powders for cleaning teeth and gums (which was done with strips of cloth): might include any of the following: powdered charcoal, salt crystals, sage, mint, cinnamon, cloves

small jars of vinegar or wine with herbs such as mint, cinnamon, or cloves, used as mouthwash

oratory—a personal prayer desk with a shelf for a Bible or devotional and a padded bench for kneeling (called prie-dieus after the 17th century)

wooden interior shutters
to cover windows at
night and in the winter

wooden beam ceilings

wall carvings or plaster
moldings of the family's
coat of arms

iron chandeliers
holding candles

iron pokers for the fireplace

a dais—a raised stone
or wooden platform in
the great hall with the
lord and lady's table

rushlights—miniature torches
made from rushes and bacon
fat or other kitchen drippings,
in iron holders—much
cheaper than candles

bronze, brass, tin, or
ceramic oil lamps

the solar—the private living
quarters of the noble family

drawbridge over a moat

torches outside a
main entrance

private chapels for the family's
daily or weekly Mass, often
with stained glass windows

dice, made from bone or
wood—sometimes loaded
by unscrupulous types

"murder holes"—slits in castle
walls to shoot arrows through

portcullis—an iron gate
lowered to close off
a castle entrance

dungeon—often
underground, but sometimes
at the top of a tower

a pole for hanging
clothes to keep them
out of reach of mice

mortar and pestle for grinding
spices and ingredients

a garden near the kitchen for
vegetables (see Tastes, below)
and culinary and medicinal
herbs such as rosemary, sage,
bay, thyme, parsley, chives, dill,
rue, fennel, and opium poppy

SOUNDS

church bells

creaking metal
hinges on doors

trumpets announcing
an esteemed person's
arrival or calling the
noble family to dinner

troubadours, singing
while playing lutes—they
might sing sad or longing
ballads, racy songs, satirical
songs, or adventurous
ballads, often in French

musicians playing harps,
psalteries (similar to zithers),
pipes (first referred to as
recorders in the 14th century),
shawms (double-reed
instruments, similar to oboes,
12th century—onward),
flutes, bagpipes, drums,
cymbals, and/or fiddles

clash of swords in
a training yard

blacksmith hammering
in the castle forge

SMELLS

smoke from fires

beeswax candles
(church, nobility)

tallow candles (everyone else)

Castile soap imported
from Spain

mint—strewn on rush floor
mats to keep pests away

chamomile—also strewn
on rush floor mats, for
the pleasant smell

lavender—also strewn on
floor mats, and folded into
stored clothing and linens

dried rose petals, also folded
into stored clothing and linens

rosewater in bowls at the table
for washing hands after meals

stink from cesspool
beneath the castle

TASTES

Foods marked with an asterisk would've been eaten most often, if not exclusively, by the nobility.

cabbages

leeks

turnips

onions

carrots

peas

beans

apples

foraged mushrooms

cheese

milk—for the young, elderly, or infirm

wine—plain, and mulled*

mead*

ale

aqua vitae (liquor)*

beef*

pork

lamb and mutton*

rabbit and hare

venison and boar*

chicken

pigeons, ducks, and geese

chicken, duck, and goose eggs

white bread*

dark rye bread (peasants only)

pickled herring (fish was especially eaten on religious "fast days" when eating meat was discouraged)

shellfish—crabs, oysters, mussels

cod in jelly, topped with almonds*

eel and salmon fritters

savory pies, made with all kinds of meats and vegetables

roasted chestnuts

walnuts

faux almond milk "eggs" and almond milk cheese for fast days* spices: pepper, cinnamon, saffron, ginger, and cloves, often used in spicy sauces*

barley porridge

pottage: a peasant stew made with barley or oats

oatcakes

candied ginger as an after-meal digestive*

dried dates and figs*

pears in wine and honey*

seedcakes with honey*

DETAILS FOR A REGENCY-ERA ENGLISH ESTATE

SIGHTS

chaise: a light carriage
for one or two people
with a folding top, drawn
by one or two horses

coach: a heavy carriage for
up to four people, drawn
by two to six horses

phaeton: an open carriage
with four large wheels, fast,
drawn by one or two horses

gardens with topiary—
perfectly clipped shrubs

Greek or Roman-style
statues in the garden

ivy climbing the walls

archery targets on a lawn

marble busts and/or
outdoor statues in the
classical Roman style

mahogany and
rosewood furniture

Chinese wallpapers

silk damask wall hangings
(and wallpaper that
looked like damask)

oak floors with
parquet borders

Turkish and Persian rugs

rugs with neoclassical designs

small bubbles and waves
in glass windowpanes

a stained glass window, maybe
with the family coat of arms

bookcases with
leatherbound books

library steps on caster wheels

tufted leather club chairs

a picture gallery—red or green
walls, paintings in gilt frames,
including many portraits

green baize doors separating
servants' quarters from
the rest of the house

white table linens

candelabras—silver,
or gilt and crystal

crystal chandeliers

cut-glass decanters and
small glasses for port

white marble fireplaces

porcelain teacups and
saucers, with flower and
ribbon motifs or Chinese-
inspired scenic designs

porcelain vases with floral
motifs and gilt accents

wooden sewing box
with brass accents and
a lid, for needlework

pianoforte

harp

a backgammon
board and pieces

a cribbage board

round convex gilded mirrors
("looking-glasses") with an
eagle ornament on top

an ivory or mother-of-pearl
fan, maybe cut to look like
lace—or a painted silk fan

bronze inkwells decorated with
gilt Cupids, Venus, dolphins,
dogs, or Egyptian motifs

a porcelain chamber pot
with a lid under the bed

damask, velvet, and
brocade curtains and
swags, often embellished
with tassels and fringe

long silk evening gloves

parasols, cotton or silk,
sometimes trimmed with
lace or fringe; black if
owner is in mourning

walking canes, wood
with ivory, horn, gold,
or silver handles

fishing rods

silver punchbowls

ebony, tortoiseshell,
or mahogany bracket
clocks (a small table
clock with a handle)

silver samovar with a spout,
used to heat water for tea

pitchers and large wash
bowls for daily washing up

copper or zinc tub for bathing

battledores—small
racquets; precursor to
badminton racquets

shuttlecocks—similar
to modern badminton
shuttlecocks

large iron cooking pots

separate bedrooms for
a very wealthy master
and the mistress of the
house, sometimes with
a door in between

scullery—a room with a stone
floor adjoining the kitchen
where pots, pans, china,
and silver were cleaned and
stored, and where clothes
and linens were washed

copper sink used for
washing fine china

the butler's pantry—a room
full of cabinets where
silver, fine china, glasses,
and fine linens were stored
under lock and key

a servant's attic bedroom

toothbrushes made out of
wood, bone, ivory, or silver

tooth powder for
brushing—in tins, or in
fancier ceramic or glass jars

bars of Pears' soap—oval,
golden, and transparent

tins of face powder made
of rice flour and/or ground
bismuth, for covering
blemishes and freckles

tins of powdered rouge

tins of Rose Lip Salve
(a tinted lip balm)

silver combs, sometimes
with pearls, to wear in the
hair on elegant occasions

bay rum—a cologne for men
that smells like bay leaves

straight razor (or "cut
throat razor") with
tortoiseshell handle, in a
leather case, for shaving

leather razor strop for
sharpening razors

boar bristle or badger
bristle shaving brushes with
handles of ivory, horn,
rosewood, or ebony

hairbrushes made of
wood or ivory and boar
bristles for the wealthy

hairbrushes made from goat
hair for the less wealthy

bedwarmers made of brass
or tin with long wooden
handles, which servants filled
with hot coals and passed
over the sheets on the bed

mahogany four-poster beds

gold, rose gold, or silver
wedding ring for a bride,
sometimes set with
diamonds, pearls, garnets,
rubies, and/or emeralds
(men didn't wear wedding
rings, and engagement
rings weren't a tradition)

vases with fresh flowers
on the mantel

rosewood chaise longues

needlework samplers in
silk or wool thread

embroidered woolwork
slippers, handmade as gifts

watercolor paints, brushes,
and easels—painting
was a popular hobby

picnic baskets

silver or gold thimbles

"quizzing glasses"—single
magnifying glasses on chains

wire-rimmed spectacles,
sometimes with tinted green
lenses, sometimes kept in
brass, silver, shagreen, or
mother-of-pearl cases

snuff boxes, made of silver,
porcelain, enamel, or gold

SOUNDS

rattling carriages

ticking clocks

someone playing
the pianoforte

cooing doves

singing nightingales
(May and June)

chiming household clocks

brass bells in servants'
quarters ringing for service

English country dance
tunes, reels, and the
occasional waltz at a country
ball—musical instruments
might include piano, violin,
flute, lute, and/or cello

TASTES

tea and toast or hot buttered
rolls for breakfast

coffee

hot chocolate

plum cake

pound cake

Queen cakes: small currant
cakes flavored with
rosewater and almonds

hot cross buns

fresh lemonade

negus: hot mulled wine
with water, served at balls

claret

brandy and rum

piccalilli: cauliflower and
other vegetables pickled
in a spicy brine

white soup: beef or veal
stock, chicken, cream, egg
yolks, herbs, onions, celery,
and ground almonds

fresh game: venison, hare,
partridge, pigeon, quail

Stilton cheese (expensive)

trays of cold meats, fresh
fruits, and/or cakes, for
guests paying visits

roast chicken

chicken and mushroom
fricassee (a creamy stew)

glazed ham

gooseberry pudding
(a baked dish)

summer pudding (a
molded dish made with
white bread and berries)

stuffed Christmas turkey

Christmas mince pie

vegetables and fruits from the garden and orchard: berries, potatoes, apples, plums

suckling pig with prune sauce

beefsteak

port (mainly after dinner, and mainly for men)

Madeira

4. ACTION

Most of us believe that "actions speak louder than words." No matter what we think or say, nothing defines who we are more clearly than what we *do*...or what we don't do. The same holds true for the characters in our stories. It's no wonder that F. Scott Fitzgerald wrote a note to himself, in capital letters: ACTION IS CHARACTER.

Screenwriters, in particular, need to tell their stories through actions as much as words. Even in a novel, when the reader has access to the characters' internal life, action is what moves the story forward.

This section includes actions characters may take when feeling different emotions. Of course, you have to think about what's right for your particular character. If you like to work on character development before you write a story, you can think about what triggers their emotions, and how they react or express them. You might want to ask questions like:

"What's their love language?"

"What makes this person angry, and how do they act when they're angry?"

"What makes them sad, and how do they respond to that?"

Sometimes this character development work can lead to great ideas for scenes.

200 SMALL ACTIONS

In any scene, you might want to use a minor action to convey certain information about the character's personality or their frame of mind. Of course, an action can also be a misdirect. A man who repeatedly pulls off his wedding ring and puts it on again may be considering divorce. Then again, he might just fidget a lot.

Many of the actions in this list are neutral. Sometimes, if you have a long conversation between characters, and it's starting to look like the transcript of a phone call on the page, you want little actions that remind the reader that these characters still have physical bodies. Most of these are everyday things that don't take long to do.

1. take a bite of food or a drink

2. take someone else's French fry, or a bite from another person's plate

3. reach for food that isn't there—in an empty bag of chips or an empty bowl

4. attempt to drink from an empty cup

5. make a pot of coffee

6. refill someone's mug or glass

7. stir sugar or cream into coffee or tea

8. stir batter in a bowl, or soup on the stove

9. cut up vegetables or fruit

10. take something out of the oven

11. squeeze hot sauce, ketchup, or mustard on food

12. shake or pound on the bottom of a bottle to get the condiment to come out

13. take out reading glasses to read a book or menu

14. move a straw of a fast food drink up and down, making a squeaky noise

15. tear the label off a beer bottle

16. put on or take off a coat or jacket

17. put on or take off gloves

18. open, close, or shake extra water off an umbrella

19. lean a walking stick or cane against a wall

20. grab onto the back of a chair or a counter for support

21. rinse out a dish in the sink

22. polish silverware

23. clean or sharpen a knife

24. light a cigarette or cigar, or take a drag

25. stub out a cigarette or cigar

26. check a phone—for messages, headlines, sports scores

27. silence a phone call or alert

28. get up to look out the window

29. open or close a window

30. open or close a door

31. adjust the thermostat, or turn a fan, a/c unit, or space heater on or off

32. put on or take off shoes

33. pull up sagging pants, tights, pantyhose, or leggings

34. pull down the hem of a dress or skirt that's riding up

35. hold up a garment in front of the body, when shopping or deciding what to wear

36. pick a flower

37. pull a weed

38. crumple up a piece of paper, a soda can, or a beer can

39. throw something away

40. toss a toy or a treat to a dog

41. pet a cat or dog

42. snap a briefcase open or shut

43. zip or unzip a bag or suitcase

44. poke a fire

45. toss a stone into a pond

46. dribble a basketball

47. bounce a ball against a wall

48. flip through the pages of a book or magazine

49. file a paper document

50. collate and/or staple papers

51. grab or flip open a note pad to take notes

52. doodle with a pen on a piece of paper

53. pick something up and put it away

54. strike a few keys on a piano, or pluck a few strings on a harp

55. wash hands or apply hand sanitizer

56. shake hands in air or wipe them on pants to dry them

57. wash face

58. rub a cube of ice on one's head or the back of one's neck when it's hot

59. mop one's brow with a handkerchief or sleeve

60. dry off with a towel

61. brush teeth or floss

62. shave

63. put on deodorant

64. put on makeup

65. check one's reflection in a mirror or with a phone camera

66. brush, comb, braid, or curl hair

67. put in or take out contact lenses

68. shelve books or put them in alphabetical order on the shelf

69. inspect books or framed photos

70. admire artwork on the wall, or ornaments on a Christmas tree

71. press an elevator button

72. ring a doorbell or knock

73. look up at a building, a tall tree, or something in the sky overhead

74. push a reclining chair or airplane seat into the reclining or upright position

75. switch a light on or off

76. light or extinguish a candle

77. cut out or tear off a coupon

78. attach something to the refrigerator with a magnet

79. fold a throw or blanket

80. fluff or arrange pillows

81. pick up a pillow and put it on one's lap

82. knit, crochet, or do embroidery or cross-stitch

83. adjust someone else's collar or tie

84. brush off someone else's coat or pluck a bit of lint from their jacket

85. do a puzzle—searching for the right piece, putting it in place, finding it does or doesn't fit

86. apply or remove nail polish

87. pack or unpack a box or bag

88. pair socks in a laundry basket

89. iron

90. water houseplants or flowers

91. smell flowers—in a bouquet or outdoors

92. put flowers in water, or change the water in a vase

93. drop something by accident

94. wipe up a spill

95. pick up items knocked off of a shelf or display in a store

96. wipe off a counter or placemats

97. feed fish

98. dip bare feet in a pool

99. toss a coin in a fountain

100. clean glasses or sunglasses, with a cloth or on the hem of a shirt

101. apply sunscreen

102. pick a piece of fruit from a tree

103. squeeze or inspect fruit or vegetables at a market

104. put items in a shopping cart at a grocery store

105. try a sample at a grocery store or market

106. check for a price while shopping

107. tap or swipe a credit card or phone to pay

108. arrange money or cards in a wallet

109. sort mail

110. open a letter or a package

111. package something for shipping

112. wrap or unwrap a gift

113. pick at the the price tag on a book or a package

114. treat or bandage a cut or scrape

115. change a lightbulb

116. sweep a floor

117. put on seatbelt in a car or on a plane

118. adjust mirrors in a car

119. flip on one's turn signal

120. grab onto a pole or overhead bar on a moving tram or shuttle

121. pull out the retractable handle on a suitcase

122. open or close a garage door, remotely or manually

123. spray air freshener

124. write or erase message on chalkboard or dry-erase board

125. flip a wall calendar over to a new month

126. refill bird feeder

127. shuffle and deal cards

128. play solitaire

129. take pills

130. fill pill organizer with pills

131. fill out papers on a clipboard at a doctor's office

132. step on a scale

133. put on or take off headphones or earbuds

134. put up or raise a flag

135. peer through the crack of a door or through closed window blinds

136. adjust the clasp of a necklace from the front to the back of the neck

137. untangle a necklace chain

138. untangle a string of lights

139. open or attempt to open a jar

140. toss something aside in frustration

141. take off a shoe to shake out a stone

142. wipe shoes on a mat

143. tap on a microphone to make sure it's on

144. shake someone's hand

145. offer a business card or a calling card

146. clap someone on the shoulder

147. playfully push or cuff someone

147. pat someone on the back

148. hug someone

149. extricate oneself from an embrace

150. exchange air kisses with someone

151. kiss someone on the cheek

152. dap someone up

153. sidestep someone walking in the opposite direction

154. squeeze past someone in a row of seats, an aisle, or a narrow hallway

155. put up a poster

156. straighten a picture or mirror on the wall

157. dial a combination lock

158. flick someone with a towel

159. plug something in

161. adjust bra straps or backpack straps

162. sniff a shirt to determine if it's clean enough to wear again

163. push away from a table or desk in a rolling chair

164. reroll a roll of paper towels or toilet paper because one unrolled more than needed

165. pound a vending machine to get a paid-for snack to drop

165. tug on a dog's leash

165. pick up after a dog

166. pop bubble wrap

167. blow soap bubbles

168. skip on a hopscotch game chalked on the sidewalk

169. trip—on a root, or over one's own feet

170. spin a quarter in its side on a tabletop

171. study a posted map—at a mall, shopping district, airport, or nature preserve

172. peer at someone else's phone—or grab for it

173. swing shopping bags in one's hands

174. jingle change in a pocket

175. pick up a coin or a shell

176. get ready to nurse a baby (pull a blouse up or down, arrange a blanket)

177. feed a baby or child with a bottle or spoon

177. bait a hook or tie a fishing fly

179. cast out or reel in a fishing line

180. run a bath

181. splash another person—with water in the sink, in a bath, a pool, or a lake

182. whittle

183. take up or lift the reins—while on a horse or in a horse-drawn carriage

184. wind or adjust the hands on a clock

185. take a photo

186. check something off or cross something out on a list

187. throw a dart at a dartboard

188. move a chess piece on a board

189. rearrange objects on a shelf

190. rifle through or clean out a wallet, purse, or bag

191. wave an object in front of another person—to tempt them or prove something to them

192. hide an object behind one's back

193. hold an object high—out of the other person's reach

194. slide a pen, a piece of paper, or another object across the table at the other person

195. put something small, like packets of sugar at a restaurant, into a purse or bag

196. give one's jacket or coat to another person

197. pull a blanket or quilt up to one's chin

198. cover a sleeping person or animal with a blanket

199. turn away/turn one's back

200. walk away

500 GREAT WORDS FOR ACTION SCENES

Fistfights and battles, chases and escapes, shootouts and swordplay, flying leaps and crashing cars… Action scenes challenge writers to create compelling choreography, arresting visuals, and visceral character reactions. Here is a thesaurus for writing scenes that will get your readers' hearts pumping. You might even find good inspiration here for the title of your next adrenaline-fueled project.

advance	blind	chase
aim	block	choke
ambush	bludgeon	chop
assault	bombard	clamp
attack	bounce	claw
bail	brace	cleave
balance	breach	climb
bang	break	cling
barrel	bullet	clutch
bash	burn	cock
batter	burst	collapse
battle	bust	collide
beat	butt	combust
bellow	careen	command
bite	catch	commandeer
blast	challenge	corner
bleed	charge	cover

cower	drag	glide
crack	drift	gouge
crash	drip	grab
crawl	drive	grapple
crouch	duck	grasp
crumble	duel	graze
crumple	elbow	grimace
crunch	electrocute	grin
crush	emerge	grind
cuff	evade	grip
cut	exchange	growl
dangle	explode	grunt
dart	face	guard
decimate	fall	hack
defeat	falter	hammer
defend	fight	hang
defy	fire	haul
deliver	flank	hijack
demand	flare	hit
demolish	flee	hoist
destroy	fling	hook
dig	flip	hover
dispatch	fly	hunt
distract	follow	hurl
ditch	force	hurt
dive	freeze	hurtle
divert	gasp	ignite
dodge	ghost	impale
dominate	glare	improvise

incinerate	paralyze	revive
jab	parry	ricochet
jam	pierce	rise
jockey	pivot	roar
jump	plant	roll
kick	plow	ruin
knee	plummet	run
knock	plunge	rush
lacerate	poke	sail
land	pounce	save
lasso	pound	scoop
laugh	propel	scowl
launch	protect	scramble
leap	pry	scrape
lift	pull	scratch
light up	pulverize	scream
lob	pummel	screech
loom	pump	scuttle
lurch	punch	sever
maim	puncture	shake
maneuver	push	shatter
mangle	race	shear
mash	rage	shield
mount	ram	shift
obliterate	rear-end	shoot
overcome	recoil	shout
overpower	reel	shove
overturn	regain	shred
pant	retrieve	shudder

singe	stagger	tense
skid	stalk	thrash
skim	stall	throb
slam	stand	throttle
slap	startle	throw
slash	steal	thrust
slice	stick	thwart
slide	sting	topple
sling	stomp	toss
slip	storm	totter
smack	straddle	trace
smash	strain	track
smear	strangle	trade
snap	stride	trail
snarl	strike	transform
sneak	struggle	trap
sneer	stumble	tremble
somersault	stun	trickle
spin	surround	trip
spit	swagger	tumble
splay	sway	twist
sprawl	sweep	unleash
sprint	swing	upend
square off	swipe	vanquish
squash	swoop	vault
squeal	take apart	veer
squeeze	tangle	whip
squish	taunt	whirl
stab	tear	wield

wrap	wrestle	zigzag
wrest	yank	zoom

NOUNS

accuracy	darkness	headlock
adrenaline	destruction	heart
agility	determination	hell
assailant	devastation	henchman
assassin	dust	ice
barricade	effort	impact
bastard	elevator	inferno
blade	enemy	instant
blaze	escape	invasion
bone	fist	jaw
bottle	flame	knuckles
bravura	flesh	ledge
brawl	focus	lightning
brick	fracture	madness
bridge	fray	marauder
bruise	fuel	mayhem
bus	fugitive	menace
chaos	fury	mud
clash	gang	oblivion
cockpit	getaway	obstacle
concrete	gore	opponent
control	granite	pain
damage	grenade	pavement
danger	gut	pipe
daredevil	hazard	posse

precision

purpose

pursuit

rain

rescue

retreat

ribs

ringleader

roof

scuffle

shadow

shards

shock

sidewalk

siege

skill

skin

skirmish

skull

smoke

socket

soldier

sparks

speed

stance

steam

steel

sternum

stone

strength

survivor

sweat

takedown

target

team

threat

throat

thug

train

tunnel

warrior

water

weight

window

wire

wound

wreckage

wrench

ADJECTIVES

airborne

audacious

badass

breakneck

breathtaking

brilliant

brutal

catastrophic

decisive

defiant

deranged

desperate

dislocated

disoriented

dizzy

effective

excruciating

exhausted

extreme

fatal

ferocious

fierce

graceful

hard

heedless

insane

lethal

malicious

massive

maximum

messy

mighty

mindless

monstrous

nauseated

nimble

perilous

pitiless

precarious

quick

reckless

relentless

resourceful

ruthless

savage

slick

solid

spectacular

stark

suicidal

surgical

swift

ugly

unconscious

vicious

Bryn Donovan

50 THINGS PEOPLE DO WHEN THEY'RE ATTRACTED TO SOMEONE…OR LOVE SOMEONE

These are ways that your characters might demonstrate their feelings—whether they mean to or not. This list includes indirect cues and obvious signs, and some indicate deeper levels of feeling than others. Some of them can also demonstrate platonic liking or love.

1. He can't stop looking at her.

2. She has trouble meeting his eyes without blushing.

3. He listens intently and leans forward whenever she talks.

4. He inquires about her living situation, or what she likes to do on the weekends…because he's trying to figure out whether she's romantically available.

5. She asks him for a favor—possibly one that involves him coming over to her place, or her coming over to his.

6. She does him an unexpected favor.

7. He asks for his opinion or advice.

8. She reads a book or sees a movie after the woman she likes says it's good.

9. She remembers how he likes his steak, or gets his coffee shop order right.

10. In a meeting or a classroom, he chooses the seat next to her.

11. She unexpectedly defends him, or his opinion or idea, in a conversation, meeting, or class.

12. He compliments her on something that she cares quite a bit about, but that nobody else seems to notice.

13. She wears something frequently or starts wearing her hair in a certain way after he says he likes it.

14. He apologizes more than he needs to for a small faux pas or slight.

15. She gives him a lot of sympathy over something small, like if he has a cold or his weekend plans got ruined.

16. They show off in front of the other person or brag about their accomplishment.

17. She stumbles over her words around him, although she is usually articulate.

18. He forgets basic things when he's around her, such as the appointment he needs to get to, or what exactly he came to her store to buy.

19. She fidgets when she's around him or plays nervously with her phone or whatever is close at hand.

20. He notices even slight changes in her expression and body language and asks her what's wrong.

21. She talks to him about something that she never discusses with anyone. Her own openness may surprise her.

22. He asks the man he likes an overly personal question…or maybe a few of them.

23. They ask a lot of questions, just to keep the conversation going.

24. He buys her a gift for her birthday, or just because she said she wanted a particular item…even though they haven't known each other all that long. He might pass it off as no big deal.

25. She plays with her hair when she talks to him.

26. He adjusts his tie when he talks to her.

27. She finds excuses to touch him in casual ways. She might touch his arm to get his attention or to guide him in the right direction if they're walking somewhere together. She might even give him a playful strike on the shoulder in response to something he says.

28. He loans her his jacket because it's cold out.

29. She warns him about bad weather, bad traffic, or a bad-tempered supervisor.

30. He sits or stands up straight when the guy he likes walks into the room.

31. He makes a joke for her ears only about the party or the lecture.

33. He laughs more loudly at her joke than she expected.

34. She smiles a whole lot more whenever he's around.

35. He tells his friend he likes her…and later, his friend makes an excuse to leave them alone together.

36. She tells her sister she likes him…and later, her sister tells him that she's heard a lot about him.

37. She shows up for a meeting with him several minutes early…even if she makes a habit of being fashionably late.

38. He frantically cleans his apartment before she stops by—or cleans out his car before he picks her up.

39. He offers to drive her or walk her home, even if it's a safe neighborhood and she's only walking a few blocks.

40. She tries to make friends with his daughter, his mom, or his cat.

41. He just happens to turn up at a place where she hangs out or visits regularly.

42. She encourages him to take a bite of her food or a sip of her drink.

43. She connects with him on social media, and likes his pictures and posts.

44. If her friends talk admiringly about other men—acquaintances, or hot actors—she doesn't join in if he's around.

45. If his friends are joking about gross bodily functions, he doesn't join in if she's around.

46. She makes more racy jokes when she's with him, even if they aren't directed specifically at him.

47. He teases her, but in a flattering way.

48. Her voice becomes ever so slightly softer, gentler, or higher-pitched when she speaks to him.

49. He invites her to a group event, such as a party or a dinner with friends.

50. She becomes visibly irritated if someone else flirts with him.

25 THINGS PEOPLE DO WHEN THEY DISLIKE SOMEONE

You may also find inspiration on the next list, "25 Things People Do When They're Angry," and the list "50 Ways to Show a Character Is a Jerk."

1. He avoids looking her in the eye.

2. She turns her body away from him or edges away from him.

3. He crosses his arms.

4. She clicks her tongue at something they say.

5. She rolls her eyes at him.

6. He gives others in the group disbelieving looks while she talks.

7. She looks at her phone when the other woman talks.

8. He shakes his head slightly when she talks.

9. He plays the devil's advocate when she expresses an opinion—even if he doesn't strongly disagree.

10. She speaks to him in a flat tone of voice.

11. He pretends not to notice that the other person has walked into the room.

12. She abruptly stops talking to friends or co-workers when he approaches.

13. He ignores her question or comment.

14. He leaves her off a group email or a group invitation. He may claim it was an accident.

15. She laughs at something he said when he was being serious.

16. She doesn't crack a polite smile when he makes a joke or attempts to be charming.

17. She pretends not to notice when he tries to shake hands.

18. He shakes the guy's hand using an uncomfortably tight grip.

19. When she has trouble carrying something, or she's picking up things she dropped, he doesn't help.

20. He switches off the music the other person was listening to, or the TV program the other person was watching.

21.She spreads a false or unflattering story about the other woman.

22. He befriends her competitor or rival.

23. She unfriends or blocks the other person on social media.

24. She accidentally-on-purpose spills something on him or on something that belongs to him.

25. He accidentally-on-purpose bumps into the guy or brushes shoulders with him in passing.

25 THINGS PEOPLE DO WHEN THEY'RE ANGRY

Your characters will get angry in the face of a real or perceived injustice. Often, this injustice is a gap between life as it is and as they believe it should be. A foolish or spoiled character not recognize small disappointments and inconveniences as a part of normal life, but rage about how unfair they are. A usually sensible character might also do this if they're upset about bigger things.

An angry response can also be the manifestation of the instinct for self-preservation in the face of a real or perceived threat. In the context of a personal relationship, anger may be mixed with hurt—*if you loved me, you wouldn't do this*.

Some of these are healthy responses to anger, and some of them aren't.

1. Take deep breaths.

2. Voice their complaints to the person who made them angry.

3. Remove themselves, at least momentarily, from the situation that is making them angry.

4. Find a distraction, such as a book, TV show, or videogame.

5. Journal about their anger.

6. Talk to another friend or family member about the situation that's making them angry.

7. Take a walk, a run, or a bike ride, or hit the gym.

8. Listen to aggressive music at high volume—and maybe scream-sing along.

9. Scream into a pillow.

10. Vent about their anger on social media or an internet forum.

11. Refuse to speak to the person who's made them angry—for an hour, or for a lifetime.

12. Respond with a personal insult.

13. Respond with sarcasm.

14. Yell at the person who's made them angry.

15. Yell at someone whose only offense was being unlucky enough to cross their path.

16. Escalate an argument by bringing up other wrongs or injustices, past or present.

17. Do a normal task with undue force. Bang the dishes when loading or unloading the dishwasher; drive too fast.

18. Leave a task undone out of resentment.

19. Abandon someone. Leave them at a party; refuse to pick them up at an agreed-upon time.

20. Intentionally throw or spill a drink.

21. Sabotage or destroy someone else's belongings or property.

22. Throw things.

23. Break things.

24. Punch a wall.

25. Become physically violent with a person.

25 THINGS PEOPLE DO WHEN THEY'RE SCARED

1. Make nervous or sarcastic jokes.

2. Verbally deny or minimize the threat.

3. Stress-eat.

4. Stay up all night—on purpose, or because they're too frightened to fall asleep.

5. Ask their partner, friend, or family member for advice or reassurance.

6. Repeatedly check for a threat. Look over their shoulder often in a crowd; frequently check inbox, online activity, or bank account.

7. Ask someone to defend or protect them—or be extra friendly to someone, or several people, who might.

8. Attempt to appease the individual or organization that poses a threat.

9. Close the windows, draw the blinds, and lock the doors, maybe double-checking to make sure they are locked.

10. Change locks or change passwords.

11. Delete social media posts, set social media profiles to private, or delete the profiles completely.

12. Delete emails or email accounts.

13. Refuse to be alone.

14. Take a different path to work or school, or leave much earlier than usual.

15. Refuse to leave the house.

16. Pray.

17. Move money to a private bank account, or withdraw and hide cash.

18. Get a big dog.

19. Claim that an attack will be met with a stronger counterattack: legal retaliation, murder.

20. Buy a weapon.

21. Train in self-defense.

22. Go stay with a friend or family member.

23. Leave town—or leave the country.

24. Hide in a room, in a closet, or behind a large piece of furniture.

25. Attack the individual or organization that poses a threat.

25 THINGS PEOPLE DO
WHEN THEY'RE SAD

Admittedly, many of these are things people *don't* do.

1. Casually and frequently insult themselves, mentally or out loud: *I'm so stupid; I'm a loser.*

2. Sleep a lot or stay in bed a lot, possibly without ever feeling truly refreshed.

3. Mindlessly scroll social media or the internet for long periods of time. This can lead to a vicious cycle, because it's likely to make a person more depressed.

4. Post sad or angry song lyrics, depressing memes, or other messages on social media.

5. Binge-watch TV or play videogames for several hours on end.

6. Zone out or have difficulty concentrating at school, at work, or in social situations.

7. Speak in a monotone and/or mumble.

8. Give monosyllabic answers to questions.

9. Overeat, or forget to eat.

10. Lose interest in hobbies or activities they used to enjoy.

11. Turn down social invitations—or accept them, but then cancel.

12. Fake a smile at happy news or happy occasions, because they're not really feeling it.

13. Make themselves laugh at someone else's joke, because they can't find anything funny.

14. Neglect their hygiene or appearance. Maybe they don't wash their hair or shave; maybe their clothes are dirty, or they wear the same outfit a few days in a row.

15. Neglect the housework.

16. Refuse to leave the house.

17. Overreact to an unkind word or a minor disappointment with anger, tears, or both.

18. Listen to sad music that expresses how they feel.

19. Drink heavily and/or use drugs.

20. Exhibit nihilistic humor, such as jokes about death, suicide, or the end of the world.

21. Give personal belongings away—this can be a red flag that someone is thinking about or planning to end their life.

22. Out of the blue, send messages to family members or friends about how much they love them—and possibly, how sorry they are that they've been so depressed. This can also be a red flag.

23. Make plans in order to cheer themselves up, such as taking a trip or going to a movie with a friend.

24. Talk to a family member or someone else they trust about their feelings.

25. Make an appointment with a therapist or mental health professional.

25 THINGS PEOPLE DO WHEN THEY'RE HAPPY

Some of these are appropriate for a character who's in a good mood or is a happy person by nature. A few are more appropriate for a character who is excited about big news.

1. *Really* smile—with their eyes as well as their mouth. The eyes may narrow, and faint lines or crow's feet may appear in the corners of the eyes. (Fun fact: in psychology, the word for a true or genuine smile is a "Duchenne smile.")

2. Drop in at a friend's office or house.

3. Pay compliments to friends, acquaintances, or strangers.

4. Make silly jokes that aren't at anyone's expense.

5. Laugh at other people's harmless jokes.

6. Coo over babies, little children, and animals.

7. Walk with a spring in their step.

8. Briskly clean the apartment.

9. Try a new recipe or a new hairstyle or makeup tutorial.

10. Play with the dog.

11. Hum, whistle, or sing along to an upbeat song.

12. Dance.

13. Laugh off or shrug off a minor annoyance.

14. Laugh off or shrug off their own small mistake instead of berating themselves about it.

15. Point out the silver lining in a setback.

16. Hug friends or family members.

17. Make fun plans, big or small, for the future.

18. Begin new projects.

19. Assume positive intentions in others.

20. Exercise. Happy people are more likely to feel like working out—which can lead to a virtuous cycle, because exercise often elevates mood.

21. Help others, in a small way or a big way. This is another thing that can lead to a virtuous cycle, because helping someone else frequently leads to good feelings.

22. Call a partner, family member, or friend to share good news.

23. Open a bottle of champagne.

24. Shout for joy, maybe while pumping their fists in the air.

25. Jump up and down.

5. DIALOGUE

Many fiction writers feel the most confident when it comes to writing dialogue, and many find it the most enjoyable thing to write. Most of the lists in this section are examples of the kinds of things people say in various situations, but I have deliberately written them in a flat and literal way, knowing you can adapt them into the unique voices of your characters.

10 THINGS PEOPLE SAY TO PERSUADE SOMEONE

If one of your characters is trying to talk someone else into something, here are ten tactics they might use. Of course, if you're trying to talk someone into something, the most effective strategy is often to make them think it's *their* idea.

1. It would mean a lot to me. (This might be followed by a specific explanation.)

2. It would mean a lot to (another person, or others in general.) (This might also be followed by a specific explanation.)

3. You owe me—I did something for you in the past.

4. If you do this for me, I'll do something for you.

5. I think you'll want to do this because you're a good person.

6. If you do this, it will benefit you. (People will admire you, you'll make good connections, or you'll learn something.)

7. Would you rather do this or that? (This can be a good strategy when both outcomes are desirable, because it still gives the other person an opportunity to choose.)

8. These are extenuating circumstances. (This argument can be made when a request goes against an established policy.)

9. It's just this one time (night, week.)

10. If you don't, you'll regret it later.

10 THINGS PEOPLE SAY TO INTIMIDATE SOMEONE

1. You will be ostracized—from your family, friend group, or community.

2. I will tell everyone something damaging about you (true or false).

3. I will make these photos, documents, or screenshots public.

4. I will sue you.

5. I will prevent you from seeing your children or other loved ones.

6. I will destroy your chances of employment or your business.

7. I will get you arrested and sent to prison.

8. I will hurt or kill you (they may go into specifics.)

9. I will hurt or kill your loved ones (they may go into specifics.)

10. You will face divine and/or eternal punishment.

25 THINGS PEOPLE SAY TO HURT SOMEONE'S FEELINGS

1. You're bad or evil.

2. You're ugly.

3. You're stupid.

4. You're crazy/mentally ill.

5. You're a failure.

6. You don't have any talent.

7. You're never going to succeed.

8. The gifts you give or your attempts to help are worthless.

9. You're worthless because you aren't able to (have children, find a job.)

10. You're fat.

11. You're weak.

12. You're a burden.

13. You're not invited; everyone is invited except you.

14. You're a terrible (child, parent, spouse.)

15. I wish I'd never met you.

16. I wish I'd aborted you; I wish I'd never had you.

17. Everyone would be better off without you.

18. They're just being nice to you because they feel sorry for you.

19. Nobody likes you; everyone secretly hates you and/or is laughing behind your back.

20. Stop crying; you're being overdramatic/oversensitive.

21. I hate you.

22. You're the reason (name) ran away/committed suicide.

23. I wish you had died instead of him/her.

24. I never loved you.

25. You will never find love.

25 THINGS PEOPLE SAY TO MAKE SOMEONE FEEL GOOD

1. Thank you—that meant a lot.

2. You're kind.

3. You're beautiful/handsome.

4. You have an amazing sense of style.

5. You're smart.

6. You have a great sense of humor.

7. I love spending time with you.

8. Things are always better when you're around.

9. I've missed you so much.

10. I'm proud of you.

11. I'm proud to be your (child, parent, partner, friend.)

12. You should be proud that you (got sober, graduated.)

13. You're a good parent.

14. You're well-spoken.

15. You're a good listener.

16. I feel safe when I'm with you.

17. You're doing excellent work.

18. You have a good reputation.

19. You deserve this (about something good.)

20. You're going to do great things.

21. I want to be more like you.

22. You changed my life.

23. I love you.

24. You're my favorite person.

25. You're perfect just the way you are.

20 THINGS PEOPLE SAY WHEN THEY'RE SAD

1. I'm just trying to get through the day.

2. There's nothing I can do.

3. I feel lost.

4. I feel numb.

5. It's so unfair.

6. I have the worst luck.

7. I'm a loser/failure.

8. I hate people.

9. Nobody really loves me.

10. I'm so lonely.

11. Leave me alone.

12. You wouldn't understand.

13. This is how I am; I can't change.

14. What's the point?

15. The world is falling apart.

16. Things are never going to get better.

17. Things are only going to get worse.

Bryn Donovan

18. I can't take it any more.

19. I'm so tired.

20. I'm fine.

20 THINGS PEOPLE SAY WHEN THEY'RE HAPPY

1. It's a beautiful day.

2. I'm so lucky/blessed.

3. This is so much fun.

4. I'm looking forward to (tonight, this weekend, the fall.)

5. I just love (lattes, board games, bubble baths.)

6. Look at that (cute dog, sunset, big tree)!

7. I'm not going to worry about it.

8. I think most people are good.

9. You're amazing.

10. I love my friends.

11. I'm going to make more friends.

12. I love my family.

13. Life is good.

14. Life is going to get even better.

15. Thank you (to someone else, to a deity, or to the universe.)

16. This is the best thing/one of the best things that's ever happened to me.

17. I feel like I'm going to burst.

18. I can't believe this (expressing wonder at something good that's happened.)

19. Let's celebrate.

20. Yes!

15 THINGS PEOPLE SAY TO CONSOLE SOMEONE

Some of these are specific to a death, and some are applicable to tough times in general. Please note that a few of these are unlikely to be comforting.

1. I'm sorry you have to go through this.

2. How can I help?

3. Do you want to talk about it?

4. It's probably for the best.

5. Everything happens for a reason.

6. Cheer up—it's not that bad.

7. Look on the bright side: at least…

8. It's so unfair.

9. This too shall pass.

10. Take good care of yourself.

11. They're in a better place.

12. I know how you feel.

13. Do you want to (go to dinner, watch a movie) to cheer you up?

14. Here's what I would do if I were you: (advice here.)

15. This wasn't your fault.

15 THINGS PEOPLE SAY WHEN MAKING SMALL TALK

Please note that depending on the characters and the situation, some of these questions might be unwelcome. One of them could also lead to a much more detailed or candid answer than expected.

1. How's your day/week/school year been so far?

2. It sure is cold/hot out there today.

3. How's work/school?

4. How's your significant other/spouse?

5. How are your parents/roommates/children/pets?

6. How was your weekend/holiday break/vacation?

7. Do you have any weekend/spring break/summer/holiday plans?

8. How about those (local sports team name here)?

9. This place is so cute/crowded/fancy.

10. Did you grow up here in (name of town)?

11. Have you watched any good TV shows/movies lately?

12. Have you read any good books lately?

13. Have you gotten the chance to (go hiking, do any sewing—whatever their hobby is) lately?

14. I love your T-shirt/backpack/necklace.

15. Did you hear the news about (a mutual acquaintance)?

25 WAYS TO WRITE FUNNY DIALOGUE

Some of these could go in my "funny plot points" list, and vice versa.

1. A character exaggerates wildly.

2. A character makes a clever and/or unexpected comparison ("this is just like…"/"you're just like…")

3. No matter what the subject of a conversation is, a character always steers it back to the only topic they truly enjoy discussing.

4. A character gives eccentric or just plain terrible advice.

5. A character regretfully confesses—to a trivial transgression no one cares about.

6. Someone speaks very seriously about a topic that most people don't take seriously.

7. Someone responds sincerely to a sarcastic question or statement.

8. A character completely misunderstands the meaning of a word.

9. Someone is cheerful or blasé in a dire situation.

10. Someone is *pretending* to be cheerful or blasé, and they aren't fooling anyone.

11. A character is rude to a person who expects to be treated deferentially.

12. A character keeps sharing very private information that nobody else wants to hear about.

13. A character asks incredibly invasive questions, as if this is normal.

14. They tell an implausible lie, and they double down on it in an even more ridiculous way when questioned.

15. They say something inappropriate or unintentionally insulting, and their attempts to clarify or make it right just make it worse.

16. They inadvertently word something in a suggestive way. Maybe they do this two or three times in a row.

17. They call someone a name—and it's pretty creative. (This is funniest if it's affectionate teasing, or if the person being called a name is more powerful and/or really deserves it.)

18. A character can't stop bragging about a very modest accomplishment.

19. A character's attempt to change the subject is comically desperate.

20. Someone expounds upon a truly ridiculous conspiracy theory.

21. Someone makes an implausible excuse for why they can't help or attend.

22. A character takes an intended insult as a compliment —or vice versa.

23. A character pretends they have never seen or heard of something that everyone has seen or heard of.

24. One character believes they're discussing one topic; the other believes they're discussing something completely different.

25. A character has been pushed to the brink, and they're going on a rant to let everyone know what they *really* think.

WORDS AND EXPRESSIONS FOR A STORY SET IN MEDIEVAL ENGLAND

Almost all of these are straight out of *The Canterbury Tales*, written in the late 1300s, but some are from other early texts, translated from old to modern English. I also drew from various versions of King Arthur stories. Some of these words are still in use today, but aren't used nearly as often. I've indicated the meaning or usage wherever I felt that it might not be clear.

Dialogue in a contemporary story set in medieval times can't be completely accurate, because it needs to be comprehensible to modern readers. By using a number of archaic words and expressions consistently and avoiding language with too modern a sound, you can achieve a convincing historical feel.

a right good steed

all matter of mirths
("all kinds of fun")

anon ("soon" or "in
a little while")

aye

Be he...? ("Is he...?")

be ware ("beware")

begone

betwixt

bid ("ask," "entreat."
Past tense: bade.)

bold of his speech

breast (a man's or
woman's chest)

bright as any star

by my fay ("by my faith")

by my troth ("I swear")

by your leave

certes ("assuredly")

chérie (endearment, to a woman: "dear," "darling")

choleric ("bad-tempered")

churlish

come hither

cursed be that day

dally

dalliance (brief sexual relationship)

deem ("consider," "judge")

demoiselle ("damsel" is an abbreviated version of this. It means "lady," and may be used in direct address)

dumb as a tree ("silent")

ere/ere long ("before"/"before long")

fain ("glad")

fair ("attractive," of a woman; also used in place of "nearly")

fellow (also "good fellow"; used to address a common man)

fie on thee (used the same way as, "screw you," "the hell with you")

fierce as any lion

for Christ's love (used the same way as, "for God's sake")

for the nonce ("for the time being")

fresh as a rose

full (used to mean "very," as in "full wise")

"God defend you/God save you (other ways of saying "God bless you")

God's teeth (a curse)

God you speed

gone to ground like a fox ("went into hiding")

grammercy ("thank you")

grievous (often used to describe news, or a wound)

haply ("perhaps")

hark ("listen")

have some drop of pity

he acquitted himself
well ("he did well")

Ho!/Ho there!
("Hey!"/"Hey you!")

hold you still ("hold still")

hold your peace ("be quiet")

I cannot say ("I don't know")

I cry you mercy ("I
beg your pardon")

I marvel that… ("I'm
surprised that…")

I pray you of your courtesy
(the same as, "if you
would be so kind")

I say not so ("that's not
what I'm saying")

imprimis ("first of all")

in no wise ("in no way")

in sooth ("to tell the truth")

in this wise ("in this way")"

"Jesú/Jesú Christus
("Jesus"/"Jesus Christ")

jolly as a pie (meaning
"jolly as a magpie")

knave (a boy or servant; may
also mean a scoundrel)

leech ("doctor")

leman (female lover
or sweetheart)

list ("want," "like")

low company ("bad
company")

lusty ("healthy," "robust")

mark me well ("listen to me")

may the Virgin keep thee safe

meseems ("it seems to me")

messires

milady

milord

mine (often used instead
of "my" before a noun)

mischance

most like ("most likely")

must needs ("need(s) to")

naked as a needle

natheless ("nonetheless")

naught

nay

never was there such another
(storm, knight, etc.)

nigh ("near"; "nearly")

no more will I
("neither will I")

of a surety ("definitely")

on the morrow

overlong ("too long")

passing ("very")

perilous

prate (a disparaging
way to say "talk")

pray ("please")

prithee (an abbreviation
of "pray thee;" also
means "please")

privily ("secretly" or
"confidentially")

red as any fox

sanguine ("cheerful"; can also
refer to a ruddy complexion)

sennight ("week")

simpleton

sirrah (used to address
a man or boy of lower
rank; an insult)

slay

slut (a woman who doesn't
keep herself clean)"

stalwart (strong; vigorous)

succor("aid")

swain (a young male suitor)

tarry

thee ("you," as an object
of a verb or preposition)

thou ("you," as the
subject of a verb)

thy ("your")

touching him
("concerning him")

treacherous

trow ("think," "believe")

trull ("prostitute")

varlet (a servant, particularly
a knight's page; by mid-1500s,
it meant a dishonest man)

wax ("grow," "become,"
as in "it waxes late")

What cheer?/What cheer do
you have? ("How are you?")

What ho? ("What's this?")

What wilt thou say?

whether he will or no
("whether he wants to or not,"
"whether he wants it or not")

whilst

whosoever

will he or nill he (same as
"whether he will or no")

with full glad heart

witless ("foolish")

woe

yea

yellow as wax

yeoman (a landowner of a
class beneath the gentry; may
be used in direct address)

yonder

your wont ("your desire,"
or "your tendency")

WORDS AND EXPRESSIONS
FOR A STORY SET IN
REGENCY ERA ENGLAND

In the first edition of this book, I had words and expressions from Victorian England, but many people told me that the Regency period would be more useful. I didn't include both, because many of the words and phrases here were still in wide circulation later in the nineteenth century. Almost all these words are still used today, but were used much more frequently in writing from this era.

Most of these are straight from Jane Austen novels. Reading those is probably the best way to get a feel for the language of the time, but in my own experience, a cheat sheet can still be helpful. I've borrowed from a few historical letters as well.

absurd

actuate (to put into action or motion)

affront (verb: to offend someone)

affront (noun: an offensive or rude act)

abominate (to hate; abhor)

affable

agitation (emotional unrest, or something that causes it)

agreeable ("he found her extremely agreeable." Also, "agreeable-looking")

ail

affliction (reason for distress; "it is a most cruel affliction")

alacrity

amiable

amiss

apothecary (one who makes or sells drugs)

ascertain (learn, by asking or observing)

asperity (harshness of tone or manner)

barefaced (bold)

bilious (unpleasant or disagreeable)

blighted (ruined; "I cannot believe his prospects so blighted forever")

blackguard (rude, foul-mouthed, or disreputable man)

bluestocking (an overly learned woman; a woman who reads too much)

by no means ("she was by no means unwilling")

to cast up one's accounts (to vomit)

candor/candid

caprice (impulse)

cast down (discouraged; "but do not be cast down")

censure

chemise (a woman's undergarment, like a loose, short-sleeved dress)

chit (a saucy young woman)

circumspect

coarse (unrefined; "a coarse complexion," "illiterate and coarse")

conception (idea; "I have no conception what you mean")

condescend

conduct oneself (behave; "he had conducted himself miserably")

content; contentment

contrive

cordiality (friendliness; kindness)

countenance (used both to mean "face" and "expression")

courses (menstrual period)

cravat (a kind of necktie for men, usually silk)

dawdle

dear me! (an interjection, like "wow" or "oh, my gosh!")

decorum

deem (judged or considered; "deemed a fool")

delighted/delightful

design (intend: "you do not design to be cruel")

detestable

diffident (shy or modest)

disagreeable

disconcerted

discontented

disgraceful

disposition (usual mood; "her disposition was affectionate")

doleful (full of sadness)

dreadful

dull (boring)

endear ("Bingley was endeared to Darcy")

entreat

esteem

estimable (worthy of respect)

exceedingly ("Elizabeth was exceedingly pleased with this proposal")

fancy (to imagine; "he fancied himself in love")

fastidious

favor (as a verb: "if you will favor me with your company")

felicity

fever (can mean a short period of enthusiasm: "a little fever of admiration")

fond ("He was fond of the country and books")

folly

for heaven's sake

fortnight (two weeks)

fortitude

forbearance

foul ("a foul temper," "foul weather")

foxed (drunk)

genteel (refined; polite)

giddy (silly and lighthearted;
"a giddy girl")

a great deal ("he had
found a great deal to
admire about her")

governess (a woman
hired to supervise the
children in a family)

guile (deceit or shrewdness)

hale (healthy, or
healthy-looking; "a hale
and hearty man")

a happy thought

heedless

honored ("I am very much
honored to meet you")

horrid (generally awful; "that
horrid Lord Stornaway")

ill-used ("she felt ill-used,"
also, "she had used him ill")

impertinent

imprudent

indeed ("indeed, you must;"
"very dull indeed")

injurious (inflicting harm;
"injurious to their fortunes")

insolence

in vain (pointless;
without success)

irksome (tedious)

la (an interjection, like
"oh my gosh;" "La! You
are so strange!")

ladybird (a kept mistress)

laudable

laudanum (liquid opium;
very addictive)

little disposed to
("not likely to")

a man of principle

melancholy

milliner (someone who
makes and/or sells hats)

misfortune

mirth

missish (overly prim)

mortified

mortifications (humiliations)

natural daughter/natural
son (daughter or son
born out of wedlock)

nervous complaint (anxiety
or depression; "She is
not well, she has had a
nervous complaint on
her for several weeks.")

no harm ("there seems
no harm in it")

notions

obliging

odious

oh Lord!

own (admit; "you must
own she is very plain")

paltry

plain (unattractive)

plump (not a negative
description)

pray (please; "pray give
him my compliments")

precedence (the right
to go first or be treated
with more honor)

propriety

provoke ("she provokes
me by her nonsense")

quit (leave; "I should resolve
to quit Netherfield")

rake (an immoral or
promiscuous man)

rapture

remarkably

repair (to travel or move;
"they repaired to her room")

reproof (criticism)

reticule (a small drawstring
handbag for women;
often silk or beaded)

right-mindedness (common
sense, reason, or decency)

sanguine temper (cheerfulness)

scrupulous

self-possession ("as
much self-possession as
he could muster")

severe ("You must not be
too severe upon yourself.")

simpleton (foolish person; "she felt she was the greatest simpleton in the world")

singular (unusual; "it is a singular case")

solace

solicitor (a lawyer who works directly with a client)

solicitude

somewhat out of countenance (visibly flustered)

spirits (mood; "his spirits were high; "she was low in spirits")

strict ("he was of strict integrity")

stricture (criticism)

trifle with (carelessly deal with)

supercilious

unexceptionable (above reproach)

unfeeling

untoward (difficult; not to one's favor; "untoward circumstances")

upon my word (honestly; "upon my word, he is nothing to me")

a very bad business (a horrible situation)

vex

vivacity (liveliness; "the vivacity which animates her conversation")

vulgar

wanton

a wit (a witty or clever person)

would it not?/would it not be...?

wretched

your affectionate/yours affectionately (a way to sign off a letter)

your faithful (another way to sign off a letter)

yours ever (another way to sign off a letter)

6. CHARACTER NAMES

The names of the characters can make a strong impression on readers, since they are usually part of the back cover copy and/or product description. In a query letter, a name that sounds "off" can give an agent or an editor pause.

GUIDE TO CHARACTER NAMING

Here are some suggestions for naming that you might want to keep in mind as you decide what to call your characters. In all cases, though, you might have a good reason to ignore the suggestion, due to some aspect of your particular story.

1. Avoid giving multiple characters names that are very similar or that begin with the same letter.

This can lead to readers getting characters confused with one another. Beginning two siblings' names with the same letter, however, might help a reader remember that they are related.

2. Use some variety in the number of syllables in first and last names.

3. Refer to characters in a consistent way throughout the story to avoid confusion.

If a character's name is Allison, but your main character thinks of her as "Allie," use "Allie" throughout the book. Don't alternate between her nickname and her given name. You might switch at some point to indicate a change in her identity or in the relationship, however. And if you have more than one point of view character in a story, a character might be known by one name in one person's point of view, and another name when in another character's point of view

4. Make the name believable for the character's age and for the setting.

One great way to come up with age-appropriate names for contemporary characters in the U.S. is to search the most popular names for the year of their birth. You should be able to easily find a list of the top 1000 names; choosing from the top 200 or so will give you a name that sounds right for their age. You can also find, on several websites, a list of the top 1000 most common last names in the U.S.

5. Be aware of common cultural perceptions of the name.

6. If you do want to use an unusual name, consider whether you want to pair the unusual name with a common name. Examples of this naming strategy include Indiana Jones, Atticus Finch, Fox Mulder, Sherlock Holmes, and Ichabod Crane. However, the character or the story may demand both a first and a last name that is unfamiliar or fanciful to most readers.

7. If you are making up names for a fantasy novel, make all the names from each community sound a little alike.

For instance, all your elves should probably have names that sound like they come from one language, and all your trolls should probably have names that sound like they come from another language. You can consider elements such as name length, suffixes, and commonly used vowels and diphthongs and as you come up with names that sound like they belong to the same culture. Simply eliminating a handful of consonants from all the names can provide a sense of unity.

For one culture in your fantasy world, all the names might be evocative real words or compounds of real words, such as nouns or adjectives describing personal traits, colors, cardinal directions, seasons, weapons, or the names of plants, animals, and natural phenomena. You can also consider names that refer to an action, such as Strider, Aragorn's moniker in *Lord of the Rings*.

8. Consider using names that are easy for most of your readers to pronounce in their heads—as long as this doesn't compromise your story. You may have artistic or political reasons to use names that your readers won't know how to pronounce. If this is the case, you might want to provide a guide to pronunciation in the front or the back of the book.

200 NAMES ASSOCIATED WITH POSITIVE CHARACTER TRAITS OR ROLES

Some of us writers like to choose names with meanings that relate to a character's personality, their talents, or what they do in the story—even if it never comes up in the story itself. Of course, "positive" and "negative" are subjective, and it's easy to see the sinister side of a "positive" meaning or the upside of a "negative" one.

In this list and the following one, I have done my best to indicate the origin of each name, but many names have more than one origin, and sometimes the origin is disputed. Many names are used in dozens of countries.

I'm using the English transcriptions for names originally written in other alphabets. Please note that the meaning of many Asian names depends on which characters are used to spell it. Also, keep in mind that in many Asian countries the surname or family name comes first, followed by the given name, although this may not be the case when the names are translated into English.

I haven't included a meaning for English names whose meanings are obvious ("Grace," for example), unless it's a somewhat unusual English word.

By the way, as an author, you don't need to worry about choosing the same character names as other writers. Even the most avid readers read only an infinitesimal fraction of all the stories that are in print.

FEMININE NAMES

1. Aaliyah (Arabic; Hebrew): exalted; ascent; going up. Also spelled Aliyah and Aliya.

2. Abigail (Hebrew: father's joy.

3. Aditi (Sanskrit): no boundaries.

4. Alexis (Greek): helper or defender. Alexios is a masculine form, used by two Byzantine emperors. Alexius is the Latinized form of Alexios.

5. Althea (Greek): with healing power.

6. Alodie (French): wealthy. "Elodia" is a Spanish variation.

7. Amalia (German): vigorous; brave; unceasing. Amalie is a German variation, and Amelia is an English variation.

8. Amara (Igbo): grace.

9. Amina (Arabic): honest; trustworthy. Also spelled Aminah.

10. Amy (French): beloved. Amée is a French variation, and Amata is an ancient Roman variation.

11. Anastasia (Greek; Russian): reborn; resurrection. Asya and Tasia are short forms of this name. Stacy, Stacey, and Stacie are English short forms.

12. Angela (Greek): angel. Angelina and Angel are variations; Angelique is a French variation.

13. Annabel (Latin): likely adapted from the word *amabilis*, meaning loveable.

14. Ariana (Latin): most holy.

15. Athena (Greek): most people know Athena as the goddess of wisdom, so it has positive associations. Because she was also the goddess of battle strategy, this name does have a dark side.

16. Audrey (English): noble strength.

17. Avery (English): counselor to the elves. Also used as a masculine name.

18. Beatrix (Latin): a variation of Viatrix, the feminine form of the male name Viator, meaning traveler or voyager. However, it might also mean "blessed" or close to sainthood (from the Latin word *beatus*.)

19. Blythe (English): joyful.

20. Bridget (Gaelic): power and strength; or, "the exalted one." This is a form of Brigid, the Irish goddess of healing, blacksmithing, and poetry. Bridie and Bree are derived from this name. Brigitte is a French variation, and Brigitta is a German variation.

21. Callisto (Greek): most beautiful. Callista and Kallista are variations.

22. Candace (Cushitic): queen mother.

23. Caroline (French): this is a feminine form of Charles, "free man," so it could be considered to mean "free woman." Carolina, Karolina, and Carol are other variations.

24. Cassidy (Gaelic): clever. May also mean "curly-haired." Also used as a masculine name.

25. Celeste (Latin): heavenly.

26. Charlotte (French): same as Caroline, above.

27. Chenda (Khmer): thinking; intelligence. This is also the name of a kind of drum.

28. Chloe (Greek): "green shoot," "the blooming," or new growth in the spring. This is one of the titles for Demeter, the Greek goddess of agriculture.

29. Claire (French): bright and clear. Clara is a variation.

30. Clementine (French): merciful. Spelled Clémentine in French. Clémence is another French variation. Clement is a masculine form.

31. Da-som (Korean): love. May also be spelled Da Som or Dasom in English.

32. Dawn (English)

33. Desiree (French): desired, wished. Spelled Désirée in French.

34. Devi (Sanskrit): divine.

35. Diana (Latin): divine. Diana is the Roman goddess of the hunt, and Diana is Wonder Woman's name.

36. Duyên (Vietnamese): a spiritual or fated connection.

37. Emma (German, English): complete; great.

38. Eromidola (Yoruban): "my thoughts have become wealth."

39. Esperanza (Spanish): hope.

39. Estelle (French): star. Stella is a variation.

40. Eulalia (Greek): speaks sweetly, or a good talker. Two early Spanish saints are named Eulalia, though it's possible they were the same person. Olaya and Laia are Spanish variations, and Eulalie is a French variation.

41. Evangelina (Greek): one who brings good news. Eva is a nickname or a shortened form, though it can also be a variation of Eve.

42. Felicity (Greek): happy or lucky. Felicia is a variation. Felix is a masculine form.

43. Feronia (Latin): the Roman goddess of the wilderness, health, and freed slaves.

44. Florence (Latin): Derived from the Latin name Florentia, this name means flourishing, blossoming, or prospering. Florentius is a masculine form.

45. Hannah (Hebrew): favored. Also spelled Hanna. The similar name Hana means "bliss" in Arabic, "flower" in Persian and in Japanese, "one" in Korean, "to glow" in Maori, and "hope" in Kurdish. It's an all-around positive name!

46. Hiromi (Japanese): generous and beautiful. Also used as a masculine name, usually with a different spelling and meaning.

47. Galina (Greek, Russian): serenity; clarity. Galen is a masculine form, which is also spelled Gaelen.

48. Gloria (Latin): glory.

49. Grace (English)

50. Faith (English)

51. Heidi (German): of noble birth.

52. Honorina (Latin): worthy of honor; dignity. Honora is a variation; Honorine is a French variation. Nora is sometimes a short form of Honora, but is more often a short form of Eleanor or a name in its own right.

53. Hope (English)

54. Imani (Swahili; Arabic): faith.

55. Inari (Japanese): successful (literally, "rice-bearer.") This is the name of the genderfluid divine spirit of rice, foxes, tea, sake, agriculture, industry, and worldly success in general. Also used as a masculine name.

56. Iris (Greek): Iris, the Greek goddess of the rainbow, was a messenger for the gods. Iris is also the name of a flower and the word for the colored part of the eye.

57. Jamila (Arabic): beauty. Also spelled Jamilla or Jamillah. Jamal is a masculine form.

58. Joy (English)

59. Kaimana (Hawaiian): power of the sea. Also used as a masculine name.

60. Kayra (Turkish): benevolence; charity. Also used as a masculine name.

61. Leilani (Hawaiian): "heavenly flower" or "royal child."

62. Lucia (Latin): light. Lucille is an English and French variation, Lucinda is a variation created by the Spanish author Miguel de Cervantes, and Lucy is a short form.

63. Maeve (Gaelic): "intoxicating woman," or "she who rules." In Celtic mythology, Maeve is a warrior queen.

64. Malaika (Swahili): angel.

65. Mei (Chinese): beautiful. (Spelled with a different Chinese character, it can mean "plum" instead.)

66. Meredith (Welsh): greatness; magnificence.

67. Mila (Russian; Spanish): as a Russian name, Mila means "dear one," and as a Spanish one, it's derived from "milagro," miracle.

68. Miranda (Latin, English): created by Shakespeare for the heroine in *The Tempest*, but probably derived from the Latin *mirandus,* meaning "worthy of admiration."

69. Nadia (Russian, Bulgarian): hope. Also spelled Nadya.

70. Naomi (Hebrew): pleasant or gentle.

71. Naila (Egyptian): successful.

72. Nayeli (Zapotec): "I love you."

73. Nia (Swahili): goal; purpose. As a Welsh name, Nia means "lustrous" or "radiance."

74. Nirina (Malagasy): wish, dream (or: desired; wanted.) Also used as a masculine name.

75. Noel (French): born on or near Christmas. Also used as a masculine name. As a feminine name, often spelled "Noelle."

76. Nova (Latin): new. In astronomy, a nova is a star that suddenly becomes brighter or becomes visible for the first time due to a fusion explosion.

77. Odilie (German): heritage. Odilia is a Latinized variation.

78. Pamela (English): all honey; sweet.

79. Penelope (Greek): weaver.

80. Paquini (Native American: Nahuatl): butterfly. Across many cultures, the butterfly is associated with flitting effortlessly from one thing (or person) to another; it's also associated with rebirth and transformation.

81. Paz (Hebrew, Spanish): this name means "pure gold" in Hebrew and "peace" in Spanish.

82. Phoebe (Greek): brilliant; shining one. In Greek mythology, the daughter of Gaia (the Earth) and Uranus (the sky) was named Phoebe. She was the grandmother to the sun god Apollo, the goddess of the hunt Artemis, and the witchcraft goddess Hecate.

83. Rebecca (Hebrew): to tie; to captivate. This name could have a darker side ("to ensnare.")

84. Renée (French): reborn.

85. Rhiannon (Welsh): divine queen or goddess. Rhiannon is a famous figure in Welsh mythology, closely associated with horses.

86. Sage (English): wise one.

87. Sara (Hebrew): princess. Also spelled Sarah.

88. Seraphina (Hebrew): "fiery one," or passionate. In Judaism and Christianity, the seraphim are high-ranking angels described as having six wings.

89. Serena (Latin): calm, serene. Serenity is a related name.

90. Skylar (Dutch): scholar.

---

91. Sophia (Greek): wisdom. Sophie is a popular variation, and Sofia is a Spanish variation.

92. Sunita (Sanskrit): well-behaved; wise.

93. Tabia (Egyptian): talented.

94. Taika (Finnish): magic; magical spell. Also a Māori male name meaning "tiger."

95. Tiên (Vietnamese): immortal; celestial being; a magical being, such as a fairy or an elf.

96. Valentina (Latin): this name sounds romantic, but the meaning isn't necessarily about love. It's derived from the Latin word "valens," which means strong and healthy. Valentino and Valentin are masculine forms.

97. Vivian (Latin): lively. Also spelled Viviane and Vivienne.

98. Xiulan (Chinese): beautiful orchid. Pronounced "shyo-lahn." In the ancient practice of Feng Shui, orchids in a home can enhance a family's fortune, fertility, and general positive vibes.

99. Zarina (Persian): golden.

100. Zoe (Greek): life. Also spelled Zoey and Zöe.

MASCULINE NAMES

1. Aaron (Hebrew): high mountain; exalted.

2. Adalric (German): noble friend.

3. Aiken (English): made of oak; figuratively, sturdy and strong.

4. Alden (English): old friend.

5. Altan (Mongolian): golden.

6. Alexander (Greek and Latin): defender of men. Alejandro is a Spanish variation, and Alessandro is an Italian variation. Alec, Alex, and Xander are short forms. Alexandra is a feminine form.

7. Amir (Arabic): prince.

8. Andreas (Greek): strong and manly. Andrew is a popular English variation; André is another variation. Andrea is a feminine form.

9. Antonio (Latin): priceless; valuable. Tony is a short form, and Anthony is an English variation. Antonia is a feminine form.

10. Archibald (French): true courage. Archie is a short form.

11. Armend (Albanian): golden mind.

12. Asher (Hebrew): happy or blessed.

13. August (Latin): derived from Augustus, this means "great; exalted," or "to increase." Auguste is a French variation; Augusto is an Italian, Portuguese, and Spanish variation. Augusta is a feminine form.

14. Baird (Gaelic): bard; poet.

15. Beau (French): beautiful; handsome.

16. Bennett (Latin, English): this is a medieval English from of Benedict, which means "blessed." Benito is an Italian, Portuguese, and Spanish variation.

17. Brian (Gaelic): hill; he ascends; mighty. This was the name of the famous Irish king Brian Boru. Also spelled Bryan, Bryon, and Brion. Brianna is a feminine form.

18. Caleb (Hebrew): This name may mean "dog" or "whole heart;" it suggests unwavering loyalty and devotion.

19. Caradoc (Welsh): a variation of Caradog, meaning amiable; loved. Cedric is an English variation. Carys is a feminine form.

20. Charles (German, French): free man or army man. This name has been strongly associated with royalty since the time of Charles the Great, also known as Charlemagne. Carlos is a Spanish and Portuguese variation, and Carl is a Danish variation.

21. Chase (English): to chase or hunt.

22. Chaytan (Native American: Lakota): hawk. Also spelled Chayton. In Lakota Sioux culture, the hawk was a symbol of speed and vision.

23. Conall (Gaelic): ruling wolf.

24. Curtis (English); courteous; polite. Curt is a common short form. Also spelled Kurtis or Kurt.

25. Daire (Gaelic): fertile; fruitful. Also associated with the English word "daring."

26. Dakarai (Zimbabwe: Shona): rejoice. Also spelled Dakari.

27. David (Hebrew): beloved, or uncle. Dawid is a Polish variation, and Davyd is a Ukrainian variation.

28. Dennis (Greek): derived from Dionysus, the Greek god of wine, as well as orchards, fruit, and theater—and religious frenzy, which has a sinister side. Also spelled Denis, the name of the patron saint of Paris. Denise is a feminine form; Denisa is a Slavic feminine form.

29. Derek (German): ruler of the people. Derived from Dederick, a variation of Theodoric. Dirk is a variation.

30. Deion (Latin): a modern U.S. name meaning God, or of God. Also spelled Dion.

31. Demetrius (Greek): lover of the Earth (literally, devoted to the earth goddess Demeter.) Dmitri is a Slavic variation.

32. Dylan (Welsh): a good swimmer. The name literally means "with the tide." In Welsh mythology, Dylan ail Don can swim like a fish. There's a tragic end to that story, because Dylan was accidentally killed by his uncle. Also spelled Dillon.

33. Edmund (English): wealthy protector or protector of wealth. Also spelled Edmond. Eamon is a Gaelic variation (rhymes with "layman.")

34. Edward (English): wealthy guard or guardian of wealth, similar to Edmund. Eduardo is a Spanish and Portuguese variation.

35. Edwin (English): wealthy friend. Also spelled Edwyn. Edwina is a feminine form.

36. Eli (Hebrew): high or elevated. Sometimes a short form of Elijah, a Jewish prophet.

37. Ethan (Hebrew): firm; enduring.

38. Everett (German, English): brave boar. Derived from the name Eberhard.

39. Ferdinand (Latin): a journey of boldness and daring. Ferdinando and Nando are Italian variations. Fernando is a Portuguese and Spanish variation. Fernanda is a feminine form.

40. Frederick (German): peaceful ruler. Federico is an Italian and Spanish variation. Frederica is a feminine form.

41. George (Greek): farmer. A famous Roman saint by this name was said to have slain a dragon. Jorge is a Portuguese and Spanish variation. Georgia and Georgiana are feminine forms.

42. Gilbert (German, French): shining promise. Gilberto is an Italian, Portuguese, and Spanish variation.

43. Gregory (Latin): observant; alert.

44. Hakim (Arabic): wise; able to pass judgement. Also spelled Hakeem.

45. Hassan (Arabic): handsome, or someone who makes things more beautiful. Also spelled Hasan.

46. Hugh (German, English): mind; intelligence. Hugo is a variation.

47. Idris (Arabic, Welsh): As an Arabic name, this means teacher or interpreter; studious. As a Welsh name, it means "passionate lord" or "enthusiastic lord."

48. Isaac (Hebrew): one who rejoices or one who laughs.

49. Jason (Greek): healer.

50. Jeremy (Hebrew): variation of Jeremiah, meaning "God will exalt."

51. Ji-hoon (Korean): wise and high-ranking, when spelled with certain characters. Also spelled Ji-hun and Jihoon in English.

52. Jonah (Hebrew): dove.

53. Jonathan (Hebrew): gift from God.

54. Justin (Latin): just, fair; righteous. Derived from the name Justus. Justine is a feminine form.

55. Karim (Arabic): generous; noble. Also spelled Kareem.

56. Kenneth (Scottish Gaelic): handsome.

57. Kevin (Gaelic): born beloved.

58. Lamont (Norse/Gaelic): predominantly a U.S. name, derived from a medieval surname meaning "law man."

59. Leonard (German): brave lion. Leonardo is an Italian, Spanish, and Portuguese variation; Leonid is a Russian and Ukrainian variation. Leo and Leon are short forms.

60. Levi (Hebrew): joined or attached; or, one who joins or attaches.

61. Louis (German, French): famed warrior. Derived from the German name Ludwig. Luis is a Spanish variant. Louisa and Luisa are feminine forms.

62. Luke ((French, Latin): bringer of light. Luca and Lucas are variations; Lucien is a French variation. Lucia is a feminine form. On the negative side, Lucifer is also a related name.

63. Lysander (Greek): liberator. Lysandra is a feminine form.

64. Massoud (Persian): fortunate; lucky. Also spelled Masoud.

65. Maximilian (Latin): the greatest. Derived from the name Maximus. Can also be spelled Maximillian. Maximiliano is a Portuguese and Spanish variation. Maxine is a feminine form.

66. Miles (Latin): soldier. This might also be derived from an old Slavic name meaning "dear."

67. Nicholas (Greek): the people's victory. Also spelled Nicolas. The names Colin and Cole are derived from this name. Nico is a variation in several countries. Nikolai is a Bulgarian and Russian variation. Nikola is a masculine variation in many Slavic countries, but more often used as a feminine name in Poland, Slovakia, and the Czech Republic. Nicole is a feminine form.

68. Noah (Hebrew): peace and rest. In the Torah, the Bible, and the Quran, Noah and his family built a giant boat and gathered up pairs of every animal to survive a flood that covered the Earth.

Nolan (Gaelic): champion; descendant of the noble one.

69. Orlando (Italian, German): famous throughout the land. Variation of the name Roland.

70. Oswald (English): godlike power.

71. Parker (English): groundskeeper. Also used as a feminine name.

72. Patrick (Latin): derived from the name Patricius, meaning nobleman. Patricia is a feminine form.

73. Peter (Greek): from the Greek name Petros, meaning stone; figuratively, stable and enduring. Pierre is a French variation, Pietro is an Italian variation, and Pedro is a Portuguese and Spanish variation. Petra is a feminine form.

74. Ramiel (Hebrew): thunder of God.

75. Raphael (Hebrew): God heals. Rafael is a variation used in many countries.

76. Raymond (German, French): counselor and protector. Ramon is a Spanish variation.

77. Rhys (Welsh): passionate or enthusiastic. Also spelled Reece. Sometimes used as a feminine name, spelled Reese.

78. Richard (German): brave ruler. This name also has deep roots in England and France. Ricardo is a Spanish and Portuguese form.

79. Ryker (German): rich.

80. Rishi (Sanskrit): poet or sage.

81. Robert (German): bright fame. Rupert is a variation. Roberto is an Italian, Portuguese, and Spanish variation. Robin is a short form.

82. Roderick (German): famous ruler. Rodrigo is an Italian, Portuguese, and Spanish variation. The Irish name Roarke may have originally been derived from this name.

83. Sebastian (Greek): venerated or revered.

84. Simon (Greek): derived from the name Simeon, meaning he who hears, or a good listener.

85. Stephen (Greek): crowned in victory. Esteban is a Spanish variation; Étienne is a French variation; Stefano is an Italian variation; Stefan is a variation in several countries. Stephanie is a feminine form.

86. Sterling (English): a former surname, this name suggests excellence or worth.

87. Takuto (Japanese): artisan, or skillful, depending on what characters are used to spell the name.

88. Tariq (Arabic): he who knocks at the door. This is also the word for the morning star.

89. Tayo (Yoruban): a reason to be joyful.

90. Theodore (Greek): gift from God. Teodoro is an Italian, Portuguese, and Spanish variation; Fyodor is a Russian variation, and Fedir is a Ukrainian variation.

91. Thomas (Greek): twin. Tomasso is an Italian variation, and Tomek is a Polish variation. Thomasina and Tamsin are feminine forms. The short form "Tom" can also mean innocent and honest.

92. Todd (English): fox; a name that suggests cleverness.

93. Trahern (Welsh): like iron. This was the name of a legendary early king of Britain.

94. Travis (English): to go across. On the negative side, some think this name refers to a toll collector.

95. Victor (Latin): winner; victory. Wiktor is a Polish variation. Victoria is the feminine form.

96. Vincent (Latin): to conquer. Vicente is a Portuguese and Spanish variation; Enzo is an Italian variation.

97. Ward (English): guard; protection.

98. Xavier (Basque): the new house. Javier is a Spanish variation.

99. Zachary (Hebrew): God remembers. Derived from Zechariah.

100. Zhiming (Chinese): having a clear goal in life. Also spelled "Chih-Ming" in English.

200 NAMES ASSOCIATED WITH NEGATIVE CHARACTER TRAITS OR ROLES

Many of these names are lovely. I've known several sweet and wonderful people with these names, and some of them are the names of people I personally admire. One of them might be perfect for a character who defies fate or the low expectations of others, or for a character with an edgy side.

FEMININE NAMES

1. Abertha (Welsh): sacrifice.

2. Acantha (Greek): prickle. The plant acanthus, also called bear's breeches, is pretty but has thorny leaves.

3. Achlys (Greek): death mist. Achlys was the personification of misery, portrayed as being covered in dirt, blood, and tears.

4. Adaliah (Hebrew): one that draws water; poverty; cloud; death.

5. Adyna (Welsh): wretched.

6. Afa (Polynesian): hurricane.

7. Agrona (English): the Welsh goddess of war, carnage, and slaughter.

8. Aja (Sanskrit): goat. No offense to goats, but most people wouldn't view this as a compliment.

9. Allegra (Italian): this name means "happy," but U.S. readers are likely to think of the allergy medication of the same name.

10. Annemie (Dutch): bitter grace. Has the bonus negative connotation of sounding like "enemy."

11. Aparna (Sanskrit): leafless. This name is associated with austerity.

12. Ara (Greek): to curse.

13. Arachne (Greek): spider. In an ancient poem by Ovid, a human named Arachne challenged the goddess Minerva to a weaving contest. After the goddess Minerva became jealous of Arachne's talent and beat her up, Arachne hanged herself. Minerva felt guilty and turned Arachne into a spider.

14. Artaith (Welsh): torment, or one who is tormented.

15. Avdima (Aramaic): loss and destruction. This is actually a masculine name, but will likely sound like a feminine name to many people because it ends in "a."

16. Bacia (Ugandan): deaths ruined the family.

17. Bailey (English): originally a last name that meant "bailiff" or "collector of debts." It's not that bad of a meaning, but it's definitely not fun.

18. Barbara (Latin): stranger; barbarian. Also spelled Barbra. Varvara is a Bulgarian and Russian variation, and Babette is a French variation.

19. Belladonna (Italian): while this means "beautiful lady," it's also the name of a deadly poisonous plant.

20. Bellona (Latin): to fight.

21. Bethany (Hebrew): this could mean "house of affliction." On a more positive note, it could mean "house of figs."

22. Binghan (Chinese): ice cold, when spelled with certain characters. On the positive side, this can be interpreted as "crystal clear."

23. Bunny (English): little rabbit. Also a short form of Berenice. For some people in the United States, this name will suggest a sexy but

dim-witted young woman, thanks to the stereotype of the Playboy Bunny.

24. Caethes (Welsh): captive or slave.

25. Candida (Latin): while the meaning is "dazzling white," this is unfortunately the name of a type of fungal infection.

26. Carmen (Latin): while the meaning is "poem or song," the most famous Carmen is the main character in Georges Bizet's titular opera, in which she is stabbed to death by a spurned lover.

27. Capri (Italian): this is the name of a charming island, but it also means either "wild boar" or "goat." A related word, "capricious," is an often negative character trait. A similar-sounding name, Caprice, means "impulse."

28. Chiku (Swahili): talks a lot. This could certainly be a positive attribute, depending on the character and the situation.

29. Daeva (Avestan): in Zoroastrian mythology, daevas are evil spirits that cause havoc.

30. Dariga (Kazakh): derived from an expression of surprise that means "what a pity!" or "alas!"

31. Deirdre (Gaelic): daughter. In Irish legends, Deirdre tragically dies of a broken heart.

32. Delilah (Hebrew): languishing; weak.

33. Desdemona (Greek): ill-fated; misery. In Shakespeare's play *Othello*, Othello accuses his wife Desdemona, strikes her and insults her in public, and later strangles her to death. Desmona is a variation.

34. Dinah (Hebrew): judged. Deina and Dina are variations.

35. Doireann (Gaelic); sullen or grouchy. Doreen is a variation.

36. Dolores (Spanish): sorrows. Lola is a short form.

37. Edith (English): happy in war; war profiteer. Edita is a Slavic variation.

38. Emily (Latin, English): the feminine form of Emil, derived from the Latin word *aemulus,* meaning an envious rival. Emilia is an Italian and Spanish variation.

39. Enyo (Greek): goddess of war and destruction; a companion to the god Ares.

40. Eris (Greek): goddess of strife and discord; sister to the god Ares.

41. Eztli (Native American: Nahuatl): blood.

42. Gilda (German, Italian): payment, tribute, or sacrifice. A short form of Ermengilda.

43. Giselle (French): hostage; pledge. Also spelled Gisèle in French. Gisela is a Spanish, Portuguese, and Italian variation.

44. Griselda (German, English) gray battle or dark battle. Griselda Blanco (otherwise known as La Madrina, or the Black Widow) was a notorious figure in a Colombian drug and terrorism cartel. Zelda is a short form.

45. Hala (Slavic): a mythological being in Slavic mythology who destroys crops with hail and sometimes tries to eat the sun or the moon, causing an eclipse. In Arabic, this name can refer to the halo around the moon.

46. Harlow (English): rocky hill; army hill. May be associated with the 1930s actress Jean Harlow, who tragically died at the age of twenty-six.

47. Helah (Hebrew): rust.

48. Hilda (English, German): battle.

49. Ita (Gaelic): thirst.

50. Jerusha (Hebrew): a possession; owned by a husband.

51. Jezebel (Phoenician, Hebrew): In the Bible, Jezebel was a princess who replaced the Israelite religion with the worship of the god Baal. She was later thrown out of a window and eaten by dogs. Her name became synonymous with false prophets, promiscuity, and even a feminine demonic force.

52. Kali (Sanskrit): the Hindu goddess associated with time, death, and devastation.

53. Kakia (Greek): the goddess of vice.

54. Katherine (Greek): this extremely popular name might be derived from the Greek word meaning "torture," but it could have other origins. There are dozens of variations, including Catherine, Katrina, Katarina, Kathleen, and Karina.

55. Kelly (Gaelic): strife; aggression. Also used as a masculine name.

56. Ker (Greek): a spirit drawn to destruction and bloody, violent deaths. Sometimes, the Keres were considered to be blood-sucking monsters. The ancient Greek poet Hesiod wrote that they were the children of Nyx, or the night.

57. Kesi (Swahili): more often a surname, this means "born during difficult times." Also used as a masculine name.

58. Kikimora (Slavic): this is the name of a house spirit in folklore. Often evil, this spirit may bring bad news and/or cause night terrors. The word is derived from a word for "scarecrow."

59. Lamia (Greek): the name of a child-eating demon, sometimes referred to as a vampire.

60. Laverne (Latin): this may mean "spring-like" or "of the spring." However, the name is derived from Laverna, the goddess of thieves.

61. Leah (Hebrew): weary; grieved. Alternately, this name may mean "cow." Leia and Lea are variations.

62. Letha (Greek): forgetful. Derived from Lethe, the mythological river in Hades.

63. Libitina (Etruscan): Libitina was the goddess of funerals and burials.

64. Lilith (Hebrew): "of the night," or "screech owl." Lilith was an ancient female demon who caused miscarriages and stole infants. In some stories, she was the first wife of Adam but refused to be subordinate to him and left him, making her a symbol of independence to some feminists.

65. Livia (Latin): envious. Related to the word "livid." Not related to the name "Olivia," which means "olive tree."

66. Lorelei (German): a siren that lured sailors to crash their ships against the rocks. Also spelled Loralei. Lurleen is a variation, also spelled Lurlene.

67. Lyssa (Greek): rage; fury. Lyssa was the goddess of anger, frenzy, and rabies.

68. Maaca (Hebrew): to press; to crush.

69. Macy (English): mace; a spiked weapon.

70. Mahlah (Hebrew): sickness; weakness. Also spelled Mahala. Mahlon may be a male form.

71. Mallory (French): unfortunate; unlucky.

72. Mary (Hebrew): bitter. There are several dozen variations of this name around the world, including Marie, Maria, Mariah, Mara, Molly, Miriam, Maia, Marietta, and Marija.

73. Megaera (Greek): grudge; the jealous one. Megaera was one of the mythological Furies who punished people for breaking oaths and being unfaithful to their spouses. In many countries, this name has been used to describe a mean woman.

74. Morana (Slavic): goddess of winter, illness, plague, and death. It also sounds like the English word "moron."

75. Morrigan (Gaelic): goddess of battle and death.

76. Myra (Arabic, Greek): myrrh. Myrrh comes from the Arabic word meaning "bitter."

77. Narcissa (Greek): although "narcissus" is a name for daffodils, it means "numbness" or "sleep," and most people will associate this name with narcissism—self-involvement, vanity, and lack of empathy for others.

78. Omusa (Native American: Minok): misses with arrows (in other words, a poor shot.)

79. Penia (Greek): poverty.

80. Persephone (Greek): to destroy; to murder. Hades abducted Persephone and forced her to live in the underworld with him for half the year.

81. Phaedra (Greek): bright. In Greek mythology, Phaedra, a princess of Crete, fell in love with her stepson, made false accusations against him after he rejected her, and then killed herself.

82. Portia (Latin): This name may translate to "door," but it may also mean "pig." Although pigs are highly intelligent and affectionate animals, "pig" is unfortunately a common insult in English.

83. Quella (English): to quell or suppress; kill.

84. Rachel (Hebrew): ewe. Sheep are lovely animals, but people who are easily led are called sheep.

85. Ranavalona (Malagasy): folded; kept aside. Ranavalona I, The "Mad Monarch of Madagascar," rose to power after the death of her young husband. She was known for her sadism and cruelty.

86. Rangda (Javanese): widow. Rangda was a child-eating demonic queen in Balinese folklore.

87. Rue (English): regret.

88. Samara (Hebrew): guardian. While the meaning is disputed, this name has sinister associations to some, thanks to *The Ring* horror movies. In an ancient story, a man tries to run away from death by traveling from Baghdad to the city of Samarra, only to find death waiting there.

89. Senka (Serbian, Croatian): shadow. Oksana is a Russian and Ukrainian variation, and Zenia is an English variation.

90. Sevdia (Arabic, Georgian): black bile; melancholy, gloom.

91. Suha (Arabic): ignored, overlooked, or forgotten. This is also the name of a star in the Ursa Major constellation.

92. Sloane (Gaelic): raid, or raider. Also used as a masculine name.

93. Taylor (Latin, English): Athough this name means "tailor," it's derived from the Latin word meaning "to cut." Of course, cutting something or someone out could be a positive thing, too. Also used as a masculine name.

94. Thana (Greek): feminine form of Thanatos, "death." In Arabic, however, this name means "praise."

95. Teleza (Malawian): slippery; dangerous.

96. Tempest (English): wild storm.

97. Tiamat (Babylonian): sea dragon; chaos monster.

98. Tisiphone (Greek): avenging murder; voice of revenge. This is one of the names of the Furies in mythology.

99. Tomila (Russian): a feminine form of Tomislav, "to torment." Tomislava is another variation.

100. Zilpah (Hebrew): weakness; frailty.

MASCULINE NAMES

1. Abbadon (Hebrew): destruction.

2. Abasi (Egyptian): stern.

3. Achan (Hebrew): trouble.

4. Acheron (Greek): river of sorrow.

5. Adad (Greek): god of storm and floods.

6. Ahimoth (Hebrew): brother of death. In the Torah and the Bible, Ahimoth is a Levite living in the time of King David.

7. Alastor (Greek): one who takes revenge.

8. Alphonse (French and German); ready for a fight. This was 20th century mobster Al Capone's given name. Alphonso is a variation; Alonso and Alonzo are Spanish variations.

9. Amon (Hebrew): invisible; in hiding.

10. Amos (Hebrew): burden or burdened.

11. Anfri (Welsh): disgrace.

12. Anwir (Welsh): liar.

13. Ares (Greek): curse or ruin. Ares was the Greek god of war.

14. Azar (Persian): fire. In the Quran, Aazar is a foolish and wicked man and the father of the prophet Abraham.

15. Azazel (Hebrew): scapegoat.

16. Bachil (Sanskrit): one who talks a lot.

17. Barrett (English): haggler; deceitful or argumentative person.

18. Belial (Hebrew): worthless.

19. Benoni (Hebrew): son of my sorrow.

20. Brady (Gaelic): a thief. It's possible this name could also mean "salmon." Braden is a variation.

21. Braen (Welsh): corrupt.

22. Bram (English): a bramble or thorny thicket; or, a derivative of Abraham. Strongly associated with Bram Stoker, author of the 19th century vampire novel *Dracula*.

23. Brennan (Gaelic): Sorrow; weeping. As an English name, this can also mean "to brand" (see below.)

24. Brent (English): this may be a place name, but "brent," meaning "burnt," was also an insult for men who had been branded on the cheek as a punishment for their crimes.

25. Brody (Gaelic): ditch or muddy place, or one who lives in or near a muddy place.

26. Brutus (Latin): heavy; stupid.

27. Burian (Slavic): near the weeds or in the weeds.

28. Buster (English): literally, someone who breaks things.

29. Byron (English): by the cowsheds.

30. Cadell (Welsh): battle.

31. Cadwyn (Welsh): chain, or one who is chained.

32. Cain (Hebrew): possessed. The most famous Cain murdered his brother. Kane can be an alternate spelling.

33. Cameron (English): crooked nose. Personally, I think crooked noses look cool, but most people wouldn't want to be addressed as "crooked nose." Also used as a feminine name.

34. Chad (English): battle. For some, this name may have a jocular quality, thanks to 2010s internet culture: a "Chad" was an desirable, successful, confident heterosexual man, often insensitive or a bully.

35. Charon (Greek): in mythology, the name of the ferryman who brings the dead to Hades.

36. Cicero (Latin): chickpea. Although this was the name of a famous orator and philosopher, this is a humble name.

37. Claude (Latin): lame; disabled. I think this feels insulting as a name because no one wants to be seen primarily in terms of their disability. Claudia is a feminine form.

38. Clay (English): frail. Clayton is a variation.

39. Črtomir (Slovene): "I hate peace" or "I hate the world." Črtomir is the hero of a famous, romantic epic poem.

40. Damian (Greek): to subdue or overcome. Damien is an alternate spelling. In the classic 1970s horror movie *The Omen*, Damien was a demonic child.

41. Dempster (English): judge. Being judgmental is often a negative quality; additionally, this name sounds similar to "dumpster."

42. Dolos (Greek): this word literally means "bait." In Greek mythology, Dolos is the embodiment of treachery and deceit.

43. Dorran (Welsh): this could mean "dark-browed," but is also thought to mean "stranger."

44. Douglas (Gaelic): dark river or black river. This meaning isn't that bad—just a bit ominous. This is a popular surname, and in 17th and 18th century England, it was more often used as a feminine name.

45. Drystan (Welsh); sadness and tumult.

46. Duman (Turkish): smoky or hazy.

47. Erlik (Turkish): a god of death and the underworld.

48. Foley (Gaelic): more commonly used as a surname, meaning pirate or plunderer.

49. Gerald (German): rules by the spear. Geraldine is a feminine form.

50. Gershom (Hebrew): exiled.

51. Geryon (Greek): the name of a monstrous giant in Greek mythology.

52. Gideon (Hebrew): the great destroyer.

53. Giles (English): servant; or, young goat.

54. Gradulf (German): hungry wolf or greedy wolf.

55. Graham (English): gravel area or gray homestead. Admittedly, this name would have a positive association for those who like graham crackers.

56. Han-jin (Korean): a rare chance for resentment.

57. Harland (French): gray land or land of the hares; also, an old nickname for a troublemaker. Harlan is a variation.

58. Ivan (Slavic): form of John, "God is gracious." To some English speakers, Ivan may have sinister overtones because of Ivan the Terrible, the first tsar of Russia, known for torturing over 60,000 people to death.

59. Jabez (Hebrew): creator of sorrow.

60. Jacob (Hebrew): supplanter, usurper, or substitute.

61. James (Hebrew): this name is related to Jacob and has the same meaning. Jacques is a French variation, Giacomo is an Italian variation, and Jaime and Iago are Spanish variations.

62. Jared (Hebrew): descent. Also spelled Jarrod.

63. Jordan (Hebrew): descend; flow down. Also used as a feminine name.

64. Jude (Hebrew): a form of Judas, famous for betraying Jesus.

65. Kasimir (Polish): usually translated as destroyer of peace. Interestingly, the argument could be made that it means "preacher of peace." Kasamira is a feminine form; Casimir is an Latin variation.

66. Kennedy (Gaelic): ugly head or misshapen head. Other sources claim it means "helmeted head." More common as a surname; also used as a feminine name.

67. Khunbish (Mongolian): not human, or weird human. This may sound like a mean name to give to your baby, but it was done to trick evil spirits into not bothering with the child. Also used as a feminine name. Khünbish is an alternate spelling.

68. Ladomir (Hugarian): trapper. This occupational name could have a sinister connotation.

69. Lamech (Hebrew): poor and lowly, or brought low.

70. Lloyd (English): gray. Many people associate this color with sadness. Floyd is a variation.

71. Maskini (Egyptian, Swahili): poor; in need.

72. Malvolio (Italian, English): ill will. Shakespeare invented this name for a pompous killjoy in Shakespeare's play *Twelfth Night* who becomes the victim of a cruel prank. Malvolia could be a feminine form.

73. Marcus (Latin): dedicated to war. This name is derived from Mars, the Roman god of war and fertility. Mark is the English variation. Marco is a German, Italian, Portuguese, and Spanish variation. Markos is a Greek variation. Marko and Marek are variations in many Slavic countries.

74. Martin (Latin, English): the same meaning as Marcus, above.

75. Melvin (English): a variation of the surname "Melville," meaning "bad town."

76. Momus (Greek): blame, mockery, or disgrace. Momus was the god of ridicule.

77. Mordred (Welsh): the meaning is disputed. In many versions of the King Arthur legend, Mordred is Arthur's nephew turned traitor.

78. Mortimer (English): dead water.

79. Nadir (Arabic): rare. In English, this word means the lowest point.

80. Nero (Latin): strong or stern. This is the name of a Roman emperor infamous for his violence and instability.

81. Ophion (Greek): serpent. Most snakes are harmless to humans, but in many cultures, they symbolize treachery and betrayal.

82. Phineas (Hebrew): serpent's mouth. Alternately, this name might have the neutral meaning of "Nubian."

83. Sergio (Latin): the Italian and Spanish variation of the name Sergius, meaning servant. Sergei is a Russian variation.

84. Shakuni (Sanskrit): bird. Shakuni is a clever and evil prince in the Hindu epic *Mahabharata*.

85. Sharar (Hebrew): enemy.

86. Soren (Latin, Danish): derived from the name Severus, meaning stern or severe. Severin is a German variation.

87. Tavor (Aramaic): fractured; bad luck.

88. Terrell (French, English): stubborn. Tyrell is a variation.

89. Thornton (English): thorn town. Often a surname.

90. Tristan (French): sad. Tristram is a variation.

91. Tucker (English): this occupational name comes from an old English word that means "to disturb, taunt, or torment."

92. Ulysses (Latin): the Latin form of Odysseus, the name for the famous hero in mythology. The name means "wrathful" or "hateful."

93. Vaughan (Welsh): small.

94. Vance (English): bog, or someone who lives in or near a bog.

95. Varus (Latin): bow-legged or knock-kneed.

96. Viggo (Norse): war; fight.

97. Vladimir (Slavic): famous ruler. Vlad the Impaler became infamous in history for his horrific cruelty.

98. Zador (Hungarian): ill-tempered or violent.

99. Zalmon (Hebrew): shadow; shady.

100. Zelos (Greek): zealous and jealous.

NAMES FROM MEDIEVAL ENGLAND

This list might also be helpful if you're writing a high fantasy with swords and sorcery. Naming trends didn't change nearly so quickly in past centuries as they do now, so it's a good resource for your English Renaissance or Tudor-era story as well.

My sources include battle histories, subsidy rolls, and *A Dictionary of English Surnames*. I also included just a few names from the King Arthur legends.

MEN

Adam	Bardolph	Charles
Adelard	Barnabas	Cyr
Aglovale	Bartholomew	Daniel
Alan	Basil	David
Aland	Baudwin	Denis
Albert	Bennet	Diggory
Aldred	Berenger	Dinadan
Alexander	Bernard	Drogo
Alfred	Bertram	Edgar
Alisander	Blaise	Edward
Alphonse	Bliant	Edwin
Amis	Brom	Egbert
Anselm	Bryce	Elias
Arnold	Castor	Eliot
Arthur	Cederic	Eluard
Balin	Cerdic	Emory

Eustace	Hubert	Milo
Everard	Hugh	Nicholas
Faramond	Humphrey	Nigel
Frederick	Ingram	Noah
Fulke	Isaac	Ogier
Gabriel	Isembard	Osric
Galleron	Ives	Paul
Gamel	James	Percival
Gareth	Jasper	Peter
Geoffrey	Jeremy	Philip
George	Jocelyn	Piers
Gerald	Jordan	Randel
Gerard	Joseph	Ranulf
Gervase	Lambert	Reginald
Gilbert	Laurence	Richard
Giles	Leland	Robert
Godwin	Leofwin	Roger
Gregory	Lionel	Roland
Griffith	Lucan	Rolf
Gunter	Lucius	Rowan
Guy	Mabon	Sampson
Hamon	Manfred	Sayer
Hamond	Mark	Silas
Hardwin	Martin	Solomon
Hector	Matthew	Theobald
Henry	Maynard	Thomas
Herbert	Merek	Thurstan
Herman	Michael	Timm
Hildebrand	Miles	Tobias

Tristram	Walter	Wolfstan
Turstin	Warin	Wymond
Ulric	Warner	
Urian	William	

WOMEN

Acelina	Bridget	Emma
Adelina	Caesaria	Etheldreda
Aelina	Cassandra	Eva
Agnes	Catelin	Evaine
Aldith	Caterina	Evelune
Alice	Cecily	Felicia
Alma	Celestria	Florence
Althea	Christina	Floria
Alyson	Clare	Genevieve
Amelina	Constance	Gisela
Amicia	Dameta	Giselle
Anais	Delia	Gracia
Anne	Dionisia	Gratia
Artemisia	Douglas	Guinevere
Athelina	Edeva	Gundred
Audry	Edith	Gwendolen
Augusta	Eglenti	Helewisa
Avina	Elaine	Ida
Barbetta	Eleanor	Ingerith
Beatrice	Elizabeth	Isabeau
Berta	Elle	Isemay
Blanche	Elysande	Isolda
Brangwine	Emeline	Ivette

Joan	Margery	Richolda
Johanna	Marie	Roana
Joya	Marion	Rosa
Joyce	Martha	Rosamund
Juliana	Mary	Roxanne
Justina	Mathilde	Sabina
Laudine	Maud	Sapphira
Lavina	Milisant	Sarah
Legarda	Mirielda	Sela
Lena	Molly	Sigga
Letia	Muriel	Sophronia
Leticia	Nesta	Susanna
Lia	Nicola	Swanhild
Lillian	Odelina	Sybil
Linota	Oliva	Tephania
Lovota	Orella	Theda
Lucia	Oswalda	Thora
Lunete	Paulina	Venetia
Magdalen	Petronilla	Viviane
Margaret	Regina	Ysmeine

SURNAMES

This list includes patronyms, occupational names, and place names. You will need to research whichever last name you choose to make sure that it makes sense for your character.

Achard	Atwood	Ballard
Alder	Auber	Barnes
Arundel	Bainard	Basset
Ashdown	Baker	Bauldry

Baxter

Beaumont

Becker

Bellecote

Beringar

Bertran

Bigge

Bolam

Bosc

Bouchard

Brewer

Brickenden

Brooker

Brooker

Browne

Burrel

Burroughs

Butler

Cambray

Campion

Campion

Canouville

Capron

Capron

Cardon

Cardonell

Carpenter

Carter

Cecil

Challener

Challenge

Chauncy

Chauncy

Cherbourg

Clarke

Clay

Colleville

Comyn

Cooke

Cooper

Corbet

Corbin

Courcy

Court

Cross

Crump

Cumin

Custer

d'Albert

d'Ambray

Dale

Danneville

Darcy

Dean

de Balon

de Beauvais

de
Bethencourt

de
Bethencourt

de Blays

de Challon

de Civille

de Coucy

de Erley

de Ferrers

de
Grandmesnil

de Grey

de Ireby

de Lacy

de la Haye

de la Pole

de la Porte

de la Reue

de la Roche

de Logris

de Lorris

de Maris

de Montfort

Deschamps

de Servian

des Roches

Destain

Dodd

Drake

Draper

Dumont

Durandal	Grosseteste	Lucy
Durville	Guideville	Lynom
Duval	Gurney	Malet
Duval	Hachet	Mallory
Dyer	Harcourt	Manners
Emory	Hauville	Marchmain
Evelyn	Hawthorn	Marshal
Faintree	Hayward	Martel
Faucon	Hendry	Mason
FitzAlan	Holland	Mathan
FitzOsbern	Holmes	May
Fitzroy	Hood	Medley
Fletcher	Hope	Mercer
Ford	Hughes	Mortimer
Foreman	Ide	Mortmain
Forester	la Mare	Mowbray
Fox	Lamb	Napier
Fuller	Langdon	Nash
Gael	Latham	Nesdin
Gary	Lea	Neuville
Gaveston	le Blanc	Noyers
Giffard	le Blanc	of Benwick
Gillian	le Conte	of Cleremont
Gilpin	le Grant	of Warwick
Glanville	le Grant	of Wichelsea
Godart	le Orphelin	Osmont
Godefroy	le Roux	Papon
Graves	le Savage	Parmenter
Griffen	Lister	Parry

Paschal	Rolfe	Vaughan
Patris	Rowntree	Vaux
Payne	Saint-Clair	Verdun
Perci	Saint-Germain	Vernon
Perroy	Saint-Leger	Ward
Peveril	Sawyer	Watteau
Picard	Seller	Weaver
Port	Shepherd	Webber
Prestcote	Slater	Wells
Rainecourt	Taylor	Wilde
Raleigh	Teller	Willoughby
Rames	Thibault	Wood
Renold	Thorne	Wright
Reviers	Tilly	Writingham
Roger	Tull	

NAMES FROM REGENCY ENGLAND

The Regency period is exceptionally popular in historical romance. This list is a good reference for any project set in England from the Georgian through the Victorian era.

The Regency period lasted from 1811 to 1820. To create this list, I used various parish records from that period. I also looked at portions of UK Census Returns of 1801 and 1821, and parts of Burke's Peerage 1826. Although these latter sources were not dated exactly to the Regency period, they were close enough to contribute to an accurate list.

Many of these names would have had nicknames, such as "Nora" for "Honora" and "Molly" for "Mary." I've only listed diminutives if they were given names in their own right. Some of the first names here are unusual for the time. Although I haven't done a quantified study, an asterisk indicates a name that showed up often in the records I consulted.

I didn't do a surname list here because it overlapped so much with the surnames in the medieval list as well as many names on lists of popular surnames in England today.

WOMEN

Abigail	Anne*	Caroline
Agnes	Arabella	Catherine*
Albina	Augusta	Cecilia
Alice*	Awellah	Charity
Alicia	Barbara	Charlotte*
Amelia	Beatrice	Christianna
Amy	Betsey	Deborah
Angel	Betty*	Diana
Ann*	Bridget	Dinah

Dorothea	Jean	Martha*
Dorothy	Jemima	Mary*
Edith	Jenny	Mary Ann*
Eleanor*	Jessie	Matilda
Eliza*	Joan	Miriam
Elizabeth*	Joanna	Modesty
Ellen*	Joyce	Nancy*
Emily	Judith	Patience
Emma	Julia	Peace
Emmeline	Juliana	Peggy
Esther*	Juliet	Phillis
Fanny*	Katherine	Phyllis
Florentia	Kitty	Phoebe
Frances*	Laura	Priscilla
Frederica	Lavinia	Prudence
Georgiana	Leah	Rachel*
Georgina	Letitia	Rebecca*
Grace*	Lilias	Rose
Hannah*	Louisa	Ruth
Harriet*	Lucy*	Sally*
Helen	Lucy-Anne	Sarah*
Helena	Lydia	Selina
Henrietta	Madalene	Sophia*
Hester	Margaret	Susan*
Honora	Maria*	Susannah
Horatia	Marianne	Tabitha
Isabel*	Marina	Teresa
Isabella	Margaret*	Theodosia
Jane*	Marjorie	Unity

MEN

Aaron	Colin	Guy
Abraham*	Cornelius	Harcourt
Adam	Daniel*	Harry
Adolphus	David*	Henry*
Albinus	Donald	Herbert
Albion	Dudley	Honor
Alexander*	Duncan	Horace
Algernon	Edmund*	Hudson
Allan	Edward*	Hugh*
Ambrose	Edwin	Isaac*
Americus	Eli	Jacob
Andrew	Elias	Jahleel
Anthony	Emanuel	James*
Archibald	Ephraim	Jasper
Arthur	Erasmus	Jeffrey
Augustus	Ernest	Jeremy
Aylmer	Evan	Jerome
Baldwin	Ewan	John*
Barnard	Ezra	Jonathan*
Benedict	Felton	Joseph*
Benjamin*	Francis*	Joshua
Brook	Frederick	Josiah
Carew	George*	Josias
Cecil	Gerard	Kenneth
Charles*	Gibbs	Laurence
Christmas	Giles	Leonard
Christopher*	Gilbert	Levi
Coape	Graham	Lewis

Lodge	Norman	Rollo
Loftus	Obadiah	Sampson
Ludlow	Oliver	Samuel*
Luke	Owen	Seth
Mark	Patrick	Shadrack
Martin	Percy	Sherborne
Matthew*	Percival	Silas
Meshach	Peregrine	Simon
Michael	Peter*	Solomon
Miles	Philip*	Stephen
Morgan	Phineas	Theophile
Moses	Ralph	Thomas*
Nash	Reginald	Timothy
Nathaniel	Reuben	Walter
Neil	Richard*	William*
Nicholas	Robert*	
Noah	Roger	

NAMES FROM WWII ERA
U.S. AND ENGLAND

If you need names for soldiers, pilots, nurses, Rosie the Riveters and Land Girls, look no further. This list can also be useful for any project set in the U.S. or the U.K. from the 1930s through the 1950s. You might even find the perfect name for an older character in your contemporary novel. Many of the names on this list are still popular today.

For the most part, names were pretty similar on both sides of the pond. The names marked with an asterisk, however, seem to have been more typical in the U.K. than in the U.S. in this period.

WOMEN

Agnes	Dorothy	Geraldine
Alice	Edith	Gertrude
Alma	Edna	Gladys
Anna	Elaine	Gloria
Annie	Eleanor	Hazel
Barbara	Elizabeth	Helen
Beatrice	Ella	Irene
Bernice	Elsie	Jane
Bertha	Emma	Jean
Betty	Esther	Josephine
Catherine	Ethel	Juanita
Clara	Evelyn	June
Dolores	Florence	Leona
Doris	Frances	Lillian

Lois	Maud*	Rose
Lorraine	Mildred	Ruby
Louise	Minnie	Ruth
Lucille	Myrtle	Sarah
Mabel	Nancy	Shirley
Marie	Norma	Thelma
Marion	Opal	Vera
Marjorie	Patricia	Virginia
Margaret	Pearl	Wanda
Martha	Phyllis	Wilma
Mary	Rita	Yvonne*

MEN

Albert	Donald	Harold
Alvin	Douglas	Harry
Anthony	Edgar	Harvey
Archibald*	Edward	Henry
Arthur	Edwin	Herbert
Benjamin	Ernest	Howard
Bernard	Eugene	Hugh*
Carl	Everett	Ian*
Charles	Francis	Jack
Chester	Frank	James
Clarence	Fred	John
Clyde	Frederick	Joseph
Cyril*	Geoffrey*	Kenneth
Dale	George	Lawrence
Daniel	Gilbert	Leo
David	Glenn	Leonard

Louis	Ralph	Thomas
Marvin	Raymond	Vernon
Maurice	Richard	Victor
Milton	Robert	Virgil
Nigel*	Roy	Walter
Oscar	Russell	Warren
Paul	Samuel	Wayne
Percy*	Sidney*	Willard
Peter	Stanley	William

7. CHARACTER DEVELOPMENT

Sometimes we get the idea for a story before we have a clue about the characters in it. Even when characters spring into our imaginations, we don't usually know everything about them at first. What's their history? What are they into? Basically, what makes them tick?

Even if your character is basically good, he or she will need flaws in order to be believable. If a character isn't perfect, that gives them some room to grow or change. Likewise, a well-written villain may have some admirable traits.

With careful thought, you can create a character who is almost as real in your readers' minds as anyone else they know in real life…a character they will never forget.

100 POSITIVE CHARACTER TRAITS

What are some of the strengths that your character relies on when the going gets tough? What's her everyday superpower? Here are lots of possibilities! In some cases, I've given an example or two of how they might play out, but of course, that will depend on your story.

1. Accountable. He takes responsibility for his actions.

2. Active. She loves biking, hiking, gardening, or volunteering. She's not so into sitting around and watching TV.

3. Adventurous. Dodgy vacation destinations and big changes in her life don't scare her. She's always up for something new.

4. Affectionate. You can always count on him for a hug, a kind word, or good-natured teasing.

5. Agreeable. You want to go to a hockey game? She says, Sure, that sounds fine. No, wait, you want to go to a cooking class instead? Okay, she says, sounds good.

6. Ambitious. He has goals and dreams, and he's positive he can achieve them.

7. Appreciative. She shows gratitude for small favors and doesn't take any of her blessings for granted.

8. Articulate. She's rarely at a loss for words. Her comments and speeches are on point.

9. Artistic. He has a flair for painting, sculpting, photography, or design.

10. Balanced. Her life is evenly divided between work and play.

11. Brave. He might be scared, or he might not be. It doesn't matter. If there's a good reason to do the scary thing, he does it.

12. Capable. He's competent and can handle situations and tasks successfully.

13. Charismatic. It may be hard to say why, but she just has a glow that attracts people to her.

14. Chivalrous. He treats women with old-fashioned politeness and gallantry.

15. Cheerful. On a regular day, he whistles while he works and never stops smiling. Even in tough times, he finds some reason to be happy.

16. Compassionate. His heart goes out to those in distress, and he does what he can to help.

17. Confident. She believes in her value and the quality of her work.

18. Considerate. He remembers your kids' names, and even your dog's name. When you miss class, he grabs an extra handout for you.

19. Cooperative. Group project? No problem. She excels at working with others.

20. Cultured. He can tell you about theater, the history of jazz, and every little gallery in town.

21. Curious. She wants to learn about everyone and everything.

22. Cute. It's not just the way she looks, but the whimsical and guileless way she dresses and acts that makes her adorable.

23. Decisive. He doesn't waste a bunch of time trying to figure out a course of action. He chooses to do something, and he does it. Bam. End of story. (Or possibly, the beginning of the story.)

24. Dependable. She never shirks her responsibilities.

25. Dignified. His self-respect shines through his words, gestures, and the way he presents himself.

26. Disciplined. He exerts self-control to meet his goals.

27. Discreet. She can keep a secret, or a hundred of them.

28. Easygoing. She's relaxed, slow to get upset, and rarely takes offense.

29. Efficient. He gets things done quickly, in the simplest way possible.

30. Empathetic. He understands how people feel and why they do what they do.

31. Empowering. She makes others feel like they can do just about anything.

32. Energetic. As long as he gets his required five hours of sleep a night, he keeps going and going.

33. Enthusiastic. She gets excited about plans, events, and occasions.

34. Entrepreneurial. She has great ideas for new businesses, and the drive to see them through.

35. Fair. He tries to make sure that no one gets shortchanged.

36. Faithful. She's committed to her spouse, and doesn't even flirt with anyone else.

37. Family-oriented. His spouse and kids come before everything else.

38. Flamboyant. He lives out loud and does everything in a big way. This may be more of a neutral than a positive trait.

39. Flexible. She can change her routine or her usual way of working to suit the situation.

40. Friendly. She goes out of her way to connect with others.

41. Frugal. She saves 15% of every paycheck, re-uses plastic sandwich bags, and never has to toss vegetables that are past their prime.

42. Funny. He always has something hilarious to say.

43. Generous. If you need twenty bucks or you want half of his cookie, he'll say yes.

44. Gentle. She has a soft, caring manner, and would never hurt anyone.

45. Good Listener. He doesn't just think about the next thing he will say. He actually pays attention.

46. Good Teacher. She knows how to explain things and encourage people as they learn.

47. Graceful. He carries himself in an elegant way.

48. Handy. She knows how to fix things around the house.

49. Health-conscious. She works out, eats right, and gets enough sleep.

50. Honest. He never takes what isn't his, and he's always truthful.

51. Honorable. He doesn't take advantage of others, and he's always good for his word.

52. Idealistic. She has hopes for a healthier planet or a better society.

53. Imaginative. She can see possibilities where others cannot, and can invent elaborate stories or worlds.

54. Independent. He doesn't mind eating alone in a restaurant. If no one else shares his opinion on something, he's fine with that.

55. Industrious. She's not afraid of a little hard work. In fact, she's not afraid of a lot of hard work.

56. Innocent. Although this trait can get people into trouble, it's often charming.

57. Intelligent. She learns things and solves problems quickly.

58. Intuitive. His hunches often prove correct, and he knows when something's off. It could be a slightly supernatural talent, or he might just synthesize a lot of disparate data on a subconscious level.

59. Knowledgeable. He's an expert in his field, or in many fields.

60. Lighthearted. She's quick to laugh at a joke, and finds many things pleasant or amusing.

61. Logical. Instead of letting emotions or fears take over, she looks at the facts.

62. Loyal. He's true to his family, his friends, and his company.

63. Meticulous. She makes sure all the small details are correct.

64. Modest. He doesn't draw attention to himself or his achievements, and doesn't especially want others too, either.

65. Mysterious. Her enigmatic appearance, words, or behavior intrigue or confuse people. This can be a neutral rather than a positive trait.

66. Natural Leader. Others look to her for direction, because she's skilled at giving it.

67. Nature-loving. He has a strong connection with animals, trees, and the great outdoors.

68. Neat. He's well groomed, and he keeps his apartment and even his car tidy.

69. Nurturing. She instinctively takes care of others and makes them feel loved.

70. Observant. He notices and recalls small details that most people miss.

71. Organized. She has a system for everything.

72. Optimistic. She always expects the best-case scenario.

73. Passionate. He feels things deeply, and expresses them emphatically.

74. Patient. She doesn't get frustrated when something or someone takes a long time.

75. Peace-making. Not only does he avoid fighting himself, but he also tries to keep others from doing it.

76. Persuasive. She could sell bikinis in Antarctica.

77. Polite. Even in strained or unusual situations, her manners serve her well.

78. Punctual. He never apologizes for being late, because he never needs to.

79. Quiet. This is actually neither a positive nor a negative trait, but it had to go somewhere.

80. Resourceful. He can cook a delicious meal out of the most random remains in the kitchen cupboard, or build a comfortable living shelter out of trash he found in an alley.

81. Restrained. Even if she's jealous, hurt, or angry, she doesn't throw a fit.

82. Romantic. Thoughtful gifts, sweet nothings, and grand gestures of love are his "thing."

83. Scholarly. She feels most at home in the classroom or the library.

84. Serene. He may be facing certain death, or even his toddler's melt-down, but he keeps his cool.

85. Sexy. Not just his looks, but his words and gestures are enticing.

86. Shrewd. His good judgment helps him strike favorable bargains and deals.

87. Spiritual. She has a deep connection with God, nature, or something else larger than herself.

88. Spontaneous. She can drop everything she's doing if an interesting plan presents itself.

89. Stylish. Her clothing choices and maybe the interior of her home show real flair.

90. Suave. He has a polished charm that serves him well in social situations.

91. Tactful. He avoids awkward questions and preserves other people's privacy and dignity.

92. Tech-savvy. When people have computer questions, he's the one they call.

93. Tenacious. Her first plan didn't work? Plan B didn't either? That's fine. She doesn't just have a Plan C—she has the whole alphabet and then some. She's not giving up.

94. Tolerant. She won't complain about the empty wine bottles you left around the kitchen or make fun of your conviction that you were abducted by aliens. "Live and let live" is stamped into her very soul.

95. Tough. Despite pain or adversity, he doesn't complain and he doesn't quit.

96. Unpretentious. She doesn't share perfectly filtered photos on social media, or try to impress everybody at the party. She's honest about herself and her life, and it's refreshing.

97. Vivacious. His warm, talkative manner makes people feel good.

98. Wise. People naturally look to her for advice, and she steers them in the right direction.

99. Youthful. He does things that you would never expect someone his age to do.

100. Zany. She's a nut. There's never a dull moment around her. This is another one that could be negative, but I think it's most often a good thing.

100 NEGATIVE CHARACTER TRAITS

Even the nicest character has his weaknesses. If he doesn't, nobody's going to like him that much – paradoxical, maybe, but true. Your nastier characters may have a whole suite of bad qualities, or they may have one that people find unforgivable.

Some of these qualities may not be things your characters can really help or change. These may make things difficult for your characters, but they are not moral failures.

101. Absent-minded. She has no idea where she left her papers, and she forgot about her meeting. She just can't seem to get it together.

102. Aggressive. Whether she's on the interstate or in a conversation, she's confrontational for no very good reason.

103. Aloof. He's so chilly, you need a sweater to go near him.

104. Antisocial. He rarely wants to take part in a conversation, let alone a friendly meal or a party.

105. Anxious. Certain situations make her nervous—or maybe it's life in general.

106. Apathetic. She doesn't take an interest in others' lives, and her own life bores her even more.

107. Argumentative. The devil never had a better advocate than this guy. Sometimes he argues just to be contrary.

108. Authoritarian. She bosses people around and tries to dictate their words and actions. Nobody had better make a move without her approval.

109.   Awkward. Although he means well, he has a knack for saying the wrong thing at the wrong time.

110.   Bitter. He feels he was treated unfairly, and he will never, ever get over it.

111.   Brusque. He seems to think talking to others is a waste of time.

112.   Callous. When she sees those sad commercials about abused cats and dogs, she doesn't even sniffle. The plight of others leaves her unmoved.

113.   Careless. If she hasn't been in a car accident lately, she's probably caused one.

114.   Childish. She expects immediate gratification and has a meltdown when she doesn't get it. She's a 3-year-old trapped in an adult body.

115.   Clumsy. He's always dropping things or running into things.

116.   Conceited. It's a wonder her ego can get through doorways.

117.   Condescending. How kind of her to deign to explain things to you.

118.   Commitment-phobic. He can't promise to show up at a barbe-cue, let alone promise to be faithful.

119.   Conformist. If all of his friends jumped off a cliff, he would do it, too, while telling everyone he's always been into cliff diving.

120.   Cowardly. She runs from even the hint of danger or risk.

121.   Cruel. Another person's pain amuses him…so much so, in fact, that he'll often cause it. This is a flaw that readers find very hard to forgive.

122.   Cynical. She greets even positive situations with a jaded attitude.

123. Delusional. He has grandiose ideas about himself and expectations for his life. This is only a negative thing when it starts to harm how he relates to others or how he pursues opportunities.

124. Demanding. As a boss, a parent, or a lover, she has a long list of things she expects you to do.

125. Dependent. He's clingy, and he can't stand on his own two feet.

126. Depressed. It may not be his fault that he's sad all the time, but it does make it difficult on everyone else.

127. Dishonest. He lies whenever it suits him, and he steals if he can get away with it.

128. Disloyal. It doesn't matter how much you've been through together or how much she owes you. She'll turn on you if it benefits her.

129. Drama-loving. He might say, "I don't want any drama," but he thrives on conflict, and his words and actions stir it up.

130. Dull. She has no particular interests and no strong feelings. She does the same things every day. She's just boring. (Readers will also have a hard time forgiving this in a main character.)

131. Foolish. She makes terrible decisions on a fairly regular basis.

132. Frivolous. He wastes time and money on meaningless pursuits.

133. Fussy. The layout of a document, temperature in a car…everything has to be "just so" for this person.

134. Gossipy. She always passes on juicy stories, whether they're true or not.

135. Grouchy. Complaining about the weather is his way of saying "good morning."

136. Gullible. You can draw her into almost any scheme or bad situation.

137. Harsh. His words, lessons, or punishments are needlessly severe.

138. Hedonistic. He indulges himself and puts his immediate pleasure above pretty much everything else.

139. Hot-tempered. It's not hard to set her off, and she yells a lot.

140. Hypercritical. As far as she's concerned, every flaw is worth mentioning, or even discussing in detail.

141. Hypocritical. For instance, she holds forth on the sanctity of marriage, and she's having an affair.

142. Ignorant. He doesn't know much about the world. If he is willing to learn, it's forgivable. If he prefers to stay ignorant, it's not.

143. Impatient. Waiting just about kills him, and he lets everybody know.

144. Indecisive. It takes her so long to choose a restaurant that by the time she does, they're all closed for the night. For years, she's been trying to decide whether or not she should leave her husband or go back to school.

145. Inflexible. He doesn't want to change his plans or routines for any reason.

146. Inhibited. She can't loosen up and be herself.

147. Insecure. He requires a lot of reassuring and flattering, and he often has the need to prove that he measures up to others.

148. Interfering. It may be none of her business, but she'll make it her business.

149. Intolerant. People who are different from her frankly infuriate her.

150. Irrational. He makes decisions based on fleeting emotions or ridiculous fancies rather than reasonable considerations.

151. Jealous. She fumes over the fact that other people have nice boyfriends, lovely homes, or good jobs, when she doesn't. It's just not fair!

152. Judgmental. Who died and left him God? Apparently he thinks *somebody* did.

153. Lazy. Her life would be so much better if she could just get motivated.

154. Lecherous. He hits on people constantly, regardless of whether they seem interested or not.

155. Loud. This is not always a negative character trait, but it certainly can be annoying in some situations.

156. Manipulative. She finds sneaky ways to get other people to do what she wants.

157. Materialistic. His prime concern is to acquire more and better stuff than anyone else.

158. Messy. His room, his truck, his hair, or all of the above are a disaster.

159. Moody. She is fine one minute and moping the next.

160. Narrow-minded. She won't listen to other points of view.

161. Obsequious. He could care less about people of lower social standing, but he sucks up to important people.

162. Obsessive. She just can't let something go.

163. Opposed to change. New procedures, circumstances, technology and trends threaten him.

164. Overcommitted. She always takes on more than she can handle.

165. Overtalkative. It's hard to get a word in edgewise.

166. Passive. Maybe he doesn't do anything evil, but he doesn't do anything to stop it, either.

167. Pedantic. She belabors all the details and formalities.

168. Perverted. He has disturbing inclinations.

169. Pessimistic. She always expects the worst-case scenario, which is much worse than anything you could have imagined.

170. Petty. He gets hung up on the slightest of slights.

171. Pompous. She's self-important and pretentious.

172. Possessive. He acts like his wife or girlfriend is his private property.

173. Prickly. You never know what will offend him.

174. Procrastinating. She puts everything off until the last minute.

175. Proud. She doesn't ask for or accept help, even when it's the most sensible thing to do.

176. Pseudo-intellectual. He takes every opportunity to pretend he is well read or highly philosophical.

177. Rebellious. This can be a positive trait, but only if there's a good reason for it.

178. Rude. Where are his manners? Nowhere to be found.

179. Sanctimonious. Why can't everyone live up to her high moral standards? That's all she wants to know.

180. Self-centered. She will rarely ask herself how her actions or a situation will affect anyone else but her.

181. Shallow. He's almost incapable of considering or discussing weighty matters.

182. Shy. He won't strike up a conversation and will get nervous if you do.

183. Smug. Her life is perfect, and she will be the first to tell you that this is all because of her good choices.

184. Snobbish. If you invite her to dinner, she'll turn her nose up at your bargain wine or your grandma's fried chicken recipe.

185. Stingy. Waitresses hate him.

186. Stubborn. Trying to get her to change her mind on anything is close to impossible.

187. Suspicious. He's pretty sure everyone's out to get him…so much so, you kind of hope that somebody does.

188. Tacky. She's too loud, she dresses inappropriately, and she has no social graces.

189. Unable to Admit Mistakes. Even when it's clear that he messed up, he'll have some kind of story or excuse.

190. Undisciplined. She can't stick to a plan or exert much self-control.

191. Ungrateful. His grandma paid for some of his college. He can't even be bothered to send her a birthday card.

192. Unimaginative. She can't envision other possibilities.

193. Vain. He's attractive, sure…especially in that big oil painting of himself hanging over his mantel. However, he isn't nearly as handsome as he thinks he is.

194. Vindictive. If she thinks she's been wronged, she will try to even the score and then some.

195. Violent. She handles disagreements by breaking dishes or breaking bones.

196. Vulgar. He makes inappropriate and gross jokes. He makes his bodily functions everybody's business.

197. Wasteful. He doesn't just spend money on things he doesn't really need…he spends money on things that nobody on earth needs.

198. Weak. When the going gets tough, she lies down and gives up.

199. Workaholic. He can't make time for his partner, his family, his friends, or anything else.

200. Whiny. Not only does he complain a lot, but he does it in an annoying tone of voice.

100 TALENTS AND SKILLS

Your character's particular strengths and weaknesses will affect how they face obstacles and how other characters feel about them. If you're putting together a team of characters to go on an epic quest, go on a heist, or just work together in an office, you'll want to give them complementary skills.

I'm leading off this list with people skills because they're applicable to so many kinds of situations. Some dubious talents and skills are included on the list, and I've included a few supernatural skills at the end. When you're considering your character's skill set, you can also draw inspiration from the hobbies and interests section.

1. persuading people

2. charming people

3. motivating people—getting them fired up

4. leading meetings

5. public speaking

6. storytelling

7. listening

8. comforting others

9. debating

10. peacemaking

11. negotiating

12. networking—may include knowing how to work a room

13. telling jokes

14. keeping secrets

15. getting people to tell their secrets

16. planning and scheduling

17. assigning or delegating

18. teaching

19. parenting

20. observation—noting nonverbal cues and other details

21. deduction—figuring out the truth based on available information

22. memorization

23. speed-reading

24. learning foreign languages

25. lip-reading

26. spelling

27. logic

28. physics

29. mathematics

30. programming/coding

31. data analysis

32. bookkeeping

33. budgeting

34. investing

35. researching

36. playing chess

37. playing pool

38. playing poker

39. counting cards

40. forgery

41. lying

43. disguising oneself

44. stealing

45 computer hacking

46. safecracking

47. "disappearing"/ not being found

48. assassination

49. cocktail making

50. waiting tables

51. being able to take a nap anywhere

52. roofing

53. cleaning

54. repairing things

55. driving (high speed; treacherous conditions; specialized vehicles)

56. piloting a hot air balloon, helicopter, airplane, or spaceship

57. sailing

58. cartography

59. navigating

60. knot-making

61. forecasting the weather

62. mining

63. gem-cutting

64. plumbing

65. stone masonry

66. farming

67. herding

68. horseback riding

69. animal training: horse, dog, falcon, etc.

70. archery

71. sword fighting

72. marksmanship

73. boxing or hand-to-hand combat

74. climbing

75. acrobatics

76. running

77. swimming

78. tracking—an animal, or a person

79. foraging

80. herbology

81. diagnosing illnesses

82. surgery

83. hair cutting/hair styling

84. doing manicures and pedicures

85. giving massages

86. doing makeup

87. dressmaking

88. leather-working

89. blacksmithing/ armor-making

90. glassmaking

91. wine-making

91. singing

92. composing music

93. video editing

94. dream interpretation

95. hypnosis

96. palm-reading

97. predicting the future

98. mind-reading or telepathy

99. telekinesis (moving objects with your mind)

100. shapeshifting

50 PET PEEVES

Sometimes you can tell a lot about a character from what aggravates them. For example, a character who never lets herself have any fun may have a strong negative reaction to an adult with a "childish" pastime. While many people are annoyed by slow walkers or slow drivers, a busy character who's always in a rush might be *enraged* by them.

1. slow walkers

2. slow drivers, especially in the passing lane

3. drivers who don't use turn signals

4. cars with lots of bumper stickers, regardless of what they say

5. loud chewing

6. loud laughing

7. murmuring, so that it's hard to understand what is being said

8. strangers wanting to converse

9. invasions of personal space—people standing or sitting too close

10. strangers making physical contact—a tap on the shoulder, for instance

11. strangers addressing one with familiar terms such as "hon," "sweetheart," or "buddy"

12. couples calling one another cutesy names

13. adults calling their parents "Mommy" and "Daddy"

14. adults being fans of something "childish," like Disney or Legos

15. someone not saying "bless you" after one sneezes

16. having to wait after showing up on time for a medical appointment or a dinner reservation

17. people arriving late

18. people who cancel plans at the last minute

19. requests to donate money

20. requests to tip for services that don't traditionally involve tipping

21. movie and TV spoilers

22. talking during movies

23. being interrupted mid-sentence

24. the one-upping of other people's stories

25. name-dropping

26. unsolicited advice

27. lying about trivial things

28. people who won't shut up about hobbies or diets

29. people who won't shut up about politics

30. people who go on and on about how wonderful their partner or children are

31. slow responses to texts

32. getting voicemails or phone calls instead of texts

33. calls from telemarketers

34. having one's name misspelled, especially in an email

35. meetings that could've been emails

36. the use of corporate jargon or slang

37. words being used incorrectly, or improper grammar

38. historical inaccuracies in books, TV, and movies

39. the sharing of false information masquerading as fact

40. not putting phones away during a meal

41. airline passengers who recline their seats all the way back

42. applause at the end of a flight or at the end of a movie

43. women wearing a lot of makeup

44. shoes worn inside the house

45. leaving socks and underwear on the floor

46. pet hair on a friends' sofa or car seat

47. signs or pictures that aren't hung completely straight

48. people who don't return their shopping carts to the proper place

49. obligatory gift-giving

50. being told, "You look tired," whether or not one is tired

50 PHOBIAS

Phobias may be learned responses, or they may be genetic. Of course, our fears are there to keep us alive, and it's easy to imagine that many of these phobias are over-active survival instincts.

This is a list of common phobias, but a character in your fiction may have developed an irrational or overwhelming fear of almost anything. I've included things that almost *everybody* fears—but for some, the fear is persistent or extreme.

A phobia can make a character seem more relatable, or it can provide an obstacle to be overcome. Your story might have another explanation for a phobia, such as a past life, a premonition, or a supernatural identity or power. Horror writers can take advantage of common phobias.

1. social anxiety disorder (SAD), or social phobia: a general fear of being judged negatively by others in social situations.

2. glossophobia: fear of public speaking. Public speaking makes many people uncomfortable or nervous, but for some, it triggers a "fight or flight" response.

3. phone phobias: fear of talking on the phone is very common. In this century, being without one's phone, or without cellular service, has also become a phobia, sometimes referred to as nomophobia.

4. hypochondria (or hypochondriasis): fear of illness. This can lead to overreactions to minor symptoms, the false conviction that one has a serious illness, or the avoidance of doctors, who might confirm a dire diagnosis.

5. trypanophobia: fear of needles.

6. nosocomephobia: fear of hospitals.

7. thanatophobia: fear of one's own death, and/or the death of one's loved ones.

8. scotophobia: fear of the dark. This is a common childhood fear, but many adults have it, too.

9. nyctophobia (or noctiphobia): fear of the night.

10. somniphobia: fear of falling asleep. Conversely, for some people, the fear of insomnia causes insomnia.

11. acrophobia: fear of heights.

12. aerophobia: fear of flying.

13. trypophobia: fear of clusters of circles. This is oddly specific, but common. People with trypophobia are likely to shudder when they see, for example, a honeycomb, a cluster of bubbles, the seeds inside a pomegranate, or a lotus seed pod.

14. claustrophobia: fear of enclosed spaces.

15. agoraphobia: this means "fear of open spaces," but it's really a general fear of finding oneself in a bad situation with no way to escape. This can make a person reluctant to leave the house.

16. enochlophobia: fear of crowds.

17. mysophobia: fear of germs and/or dirt.

18. mycophobia: fear of mold and fungi.

19. amaxophobia (or hamaxophobia): fear of driving. Some people also have a fear of riding in a car.

20. arachnophobia: fear of spiders.

21. ophidiophobia: fear of snakes.

22. katsaridaphobia: fear of cockroaches. Some people report being specifically afraid of a cockroach crawling on them while they are asleep.

23. lepidopterophobia: fear of moths and butterflies. Some people are only afraid of moths and don't mind butterflies.

24. apiphobia (or melissophobia): a fear of bees and other insects that sting.

25. thalassophobia: fear of deep bodies of water.

26. aquaphobia: fear of drowning.

27. submechanophobia: fear of submerged or partly submerged human-made objects, including shipwrecks and the underside of boats.

28. swimming pool phobias: many people are afraid of swimming pools with lane lines (which may be related to the previous phobia), or afraid of pool drains. Some experience the irrational fear that that sharks or other creatures lurk below the surface in a swimming pool, especially at night.

29. emetophobia: fear of vomiting, or seeing or hearing someone else vomit.

30. tokophobia: fear of pregnancy and childbirth.

31. cynophobia: fear of dogs.

32. toilet phobias: there are several varieties here, including the fear of not being able to get to a toilet in time, the fear of clogging a toilet, and the fear that something that doesn't belong in a toilet will be there, such as a snake or a rat. Many children are also frightened by the sound of a flushing toilet.

33. globophobia: fear of balloons. People may be afraid of the sound of inflated balloons popping, or they may be afraid of balloons in general. This contemporary phobia isn't as rare as one might think.

34. gephyrophobia: fear of bridges and tunnels.

35. catoptrophia: fear of mirrors.

36. scopophobia: fear of being stared at.

37. documentary phobia: a specific, contemporary variation of the phobia above. Many people grapple with the irrational fear that they are the unwitting subject of a reality TV show or documentary. The conviction that this is truly the case is sometimes referred to as Truman Show delusion or Truman Syndrome, after the 1998 movie *The Truman Show.*

38. pyrophobia: fear of fire.

39. metathesiophobia: fear of change.

40. atychiphobia: fear of failure.

41. disposophobia: fear of getting rid of things. Hoarding disorders, which are fairly common, can be caused by this phobia.

42. ataxophobia: fear of messiness and disorder.

43. astraphobia: fear of thunder and lightning.

44. lilapsophobia: fear of tornadoes and hurricanes.

45. obesophobia: fear of gaining weight.

46. genophobia (or eratophobia): fear of sex.

47. gynophobia: fear of women.

48. androphobia: fear of men.

49. pedophobia: fear of children.

50. apocalypse anxiety (or doomsday phobia): fear of the world ending, a mass extinction event, or global societal collapse.

50 HABITS

If you know what some of your character's habits are, it'll be easier to know how to show them in action in different scenes. Certain habits may also be the difference between who your character is and who they want to be. I tried to focus more here on physical and social habits than mental habits.

1. drinking coffee

2. drinking alcohol

3. drinking water frequently throughout the day—maybe carrying a water bottle or travel cup

4. mindless snacking

5. skipping breakfast

6. eating a certain food at least a few times a week—maybe at a certain time of day

7. smoking

8. gum chewing

9. getting up early

10. staying up late

11. sleepwalking

12. praying at a certain time of day or night

13. meditating

14. making the bed in the morning

15. doing a skin care routine in the morning and/or the evening

16. singing in the shower

17. going to the gym or working out at home

18. taking a walk or walking the dog at a certain time of day or night

19. doing extra office work at home after dinner

20. procrastinating

21. biting nails or cuticles

22. interrupting others

23. gossiping

24. complaining

25. exaggerating

26. bragging

27. complimenting others

28. making goofy jokes or puns

29. striking up friendly conversations with strangers

30. arguing with strangers online

31. jumping to conclusions or rushing to judgment about others

32. tugging at hair, especially when stressed

33. grinding one's teeth, especially when stressed

34. listening to podcasts—maybe of a certain kind

35. binge-watching TV—maybe a certain kind of show

36. scrolling or watching videos in bed before falling asleep

37. playing video games or mobile games

38. gambling

39. taking pills or doing drugs

40. spending beyond one's means

41. doing the dishes or laundry at a certain time of day

42. making to-do lists…realistic or unrealistic

43. pausing to stretch several times a day, if they work in an office

44. being chronically early or chronically late

45. wearing sandals or shorts for most of the year—even when it's cold

46. reading at a certain time—lunch hour, before bed

47. keeping a diary

48. calling or texting a family member or friend once a week, or every day

49. texting with a partner or loved one throughout the day

50. talking out loud to oneself or to a pet when no one else is around

25 LOW-PAYING JOBS

Many more people work at low-paying jobs than high-paying ones, and it's easy to root for a main character who's working hard at a low-paying job. This list and the next one aren't necessarily in order of salaries, since those can vary quite a bit.

1. entry-level retail salesperson

2. fast food worker

3. cashier

4. customer service representative

5. restaurant host/hostess

6. prep cook

7. cook

8. dishwasher

9. home health or personal care aide

10. maid or housekeeper

11. janitor or cleaner

12. parking lot attendant

13. hotel or motel clerk

14. child care worker

15. theater usher

16. dry cleaning worker

17. amusement park attendant

18. shampooer at a hair salon

19. school bus monitors

20. ambulance driver (non-EMT)

21. telemarketer

22. nail technician (giving manicures and pedicures)

23. floral designer

24. baker

25. grocery worker

25 POTENTIALLY HIGH-PAYING JOBS

The size of the company, the metropolitan area, and the character's experience will all likely affect how much they make.

1. company founder/entrepreneur

2. psychiatrist

3. chief executive officer

4. obstetrician/gynecologist

5. airline pilot

6. corporate lawyer

7. criminal lawyer

8. emergency room doctor

9. dentist

10. chief financial officer

11. head of a large advertising agency

12. senior financial advisor

13. vice president, information security (cybersecurity)

14. real estate investor

15. pediatrician

16. chief operating officer

17. investment banker

18. principal software architect

19. head of distribution, consumer goods or entertainment

20. surgeon

21. chief technology officer

22. ophthalmologist

23. luxury real estate agent

24. chief marketing officer

25. cardiologist

50 JOBS THAT SOUND
FUN OR EXCITING

All jobs have their own challenges, and our romanticized ideas of some careers may be very different from the reality. However, these are careers that many people idealize, thinking "I bet that would be amazing," or "I bet I would be great at that."

1. entrepreneur/ company founder

2. professional athlete

3. sports commentator/ journalist

4. pastry chef/bakery owner

5. coffee shop owner

6. bookstore owner

7. librarian

8. game developer

9. tour guide

10. wilderness guide

11. park ranger

12. surfing instructor

13. movie or TV star

14. movie director

15. rock star, pop star, or famous rapper

16. music producer

17. fashion designer

18. stylist or hair and makeup artist to celebrities

19. model

20. influencer

21. podcaster

22. stand-up comedian

23. architect

24. interior designer or decorator

25. winery or brewery owner

26. professor

27. schoolteacher

28. archeologist

29. paleontologist

29. marine biologist

30. caretaker at a wildlife sanctuary

31. manager of an animal shelter or pet rescue organization

32. floral designer/ flower shop owner

33. photographer

34. artist

35. president or other high-ranking politician

36. detective or private investigator

37. intelligence officer/spy

39. astronaut

41. helicopter or airline pilot

42. pharmaceutical scientist, discovering new cures

43. restaurant owner

44. inn or bed and breakfast owner

45. tree farm owner: Christmas trees, fruit trees, or maple trees for syrup

46. homesteader

47. stay-at-home parent

48. animator

49. comic artist/creator

50. author

50 COMMON HOBBIES AND INTERESTS IN THE U.S.

Our passions are a crucial part of who we are. Sometimes, a character's interests and how they spend their free time can tell readers even more about them than their occupation.

1. Watching movies.

Most people do this, but some people are passionate about movies. A character might love a certain genre, or they might be able to tell people all about productions and trivia.

2. Reading.

I also listed this in the habits section. For some people, this is a serious hobby. They might set goals for the numbers of books they read every year, and they might join book clubs to discover new books and discuss them.

3. Travel.

Your character may have the passion and the means to explore global destinations. They may be a digital nomad, living abroad for months at a time. Alternately, they may find adventure through thrifty road trips.

4. Cooking.

5. Baking.

6. Playing sports.

Of course, this covers a lot of different hobbies. Your character doesn't have to possess incredible skills (although they might) to enjoy getting out on the golf course, playing on a softball team, or spending time on the pickleball court.

7. Watching sports.

If your character is a superfan, they may often be found at a high school football stadium, a college basketball arena, or a major league ballpark. They might enjoy tailgating, meeting with friends at local sports bars, having people over to watch the game, or participating in fantasy leagues.

8. Playing board games.

"Game night" with friends or family may be a weekly fixture in your character's life.

9. Working jigsaw puzzles.

10. Photography.

Some people take a photo every day to document their lives, share lots of selfies, or seek out impressive photo opportunities.

11. Content creation.

Your character might put a lot of effort into a social media channel. It might be just for fun, or it might be a side hustle.

12. Shopping.

Almost everyone has to shop, but you might have a character who delights in finding rare items, great bargains, or unique accessories.

13. Sewing.

Making clothes, quilts, or smaller projects is a very popular hobby.

14. Knitting or crocheting.

15. Gardening.

Your character might grow flowers, food, or both. If they live in the city, they might have a plot at a local community garden.

16. Home décor or home improvement.

17. Fishing.

18. Hunting.

19. Archery.

20. Running.

Maybe your character enjoys going on short jogs around the neighborhood, or maybe they're training for a marathon.

21. Going to church.

This is more of a lifestyle than a hobby. Besides attending regular services, your character might attend Bible studies or fellowship groups, teach Sunday school, participate in projects through the church that help the community, or sing in the choir.

22. Volunteering.

Your character might be a regular at the local food bank or the animal shelter.

23. Going to the gym.

Whether they're into lifting weights or taking fitness classes, this might be a regular part of your character's life.

24. Yoga.

25. Swimming.

26. Surfing.

27. Woodworking.

28. Pottery.

29. Making jewelry.

30. Riding a motorcycle.

This might be a solitary pastime, or your character might be in a motorcycle club.

31. Riding a bicycle.

Again, this might be done alone or as a social activity—with a spouse, the whole family, or friends.

32. Camping.

A character who loves the great outdoors is likely to find some adventure.

33. Hiking.

34. Geocaching.

If your character is into this, they'll use GPS to find objects that others have hidden.

35. Home beer brewing.

36. Candle-making.

Decorating candles in various ways, such as painting them with acrylic paints, is a related hobby.

37. Calligraphy.

38. Drawing and painting.

39. Sculpture.

They could make small or large-scale creations, with clay, wood, metal, or found materials.

40. Playing a musical instrument.

In the United States, the piano is by far the most popular choice here. The guitar is the second most popular, and there are many people who play the violin, the saxophone, or the ukelele.

41. Playing poker.

Your character might go to casinos, enter competitive tournaments, or just have a game with friends every Friday night.

42. Boating.

43. Horseback riding.

If your character owns a horse, it may be a big part of their identity.

44. Genealogy.

If they're really into researching his family tree, it may lead him to visiting county archives or distant cemeteries and discovering surprising things about his ancestors.

45. Political activism.

This is more of an interest. Your character might support a candidate, a party, or a cause by volunteering or attending meetings and rallies. They might call or write letters to their leaders, participate in protests, or take part in voter registration drives.

46. Collecting.

There is no end of things that people love to collect, but they include coins, stamps, Christmas ornaments, baseball cards, comic books, toys, and certain types of figurines, including action figures.

47. Coaching.

Your character might coach their own child's sports team or be involved in a kids' sports program in their community.

48. Clubbing.

This is another one of those things that's more of a lifestyle than a hobby. Your character might love meeting new people and cutting loose. They might love cocktails a little too much, or they might just love dancing.

49. Entertaining.

Hosting dinner parties, cocktail hours, and big bashes may be your character's mission in life. Sounds like fun!

50. Writing.

Many people write poetry, stories, or fanfiction. They might also write in a journal regularly.

75 PAST TRAUMAS

One of my favorite poets, Robert Hass, began his poem "Meditation at Lagunitas" with these lines: "All the new thinking is about loss./In this it resembles all the old thinking."

Nobody gets through life without tragedies. Sometimes we forget how ubiquitous they are, because people don't always discuss them. The most successful, attractive, popular, and competent people still have heartbreak in their pasts. The difficulties your character faced in the past may or may not play a large role in your story. Either way, they will affect her personality and the way she deals with immediate challenges.

The items on this list range from upsetting to seriously damaging—and of course, different characters would respond differently to any of them. They are in no particular order. Although I made this list with backstories in mind, you may find inspiration here for a main plot.

A character's past trauma may affect her in many different ways. She may be unwilling to try or take risks in some area of her life. She may lack confidence or self-esteem. It may have resulted in a low-level depression, If she has post-traumatic stress disorder, she may experience bad dreams or flashbacks about the event. When something reminds her of it, her heartbeat and her breathing may accelerate with panic.

No matter how awful your character's past is, you can write her into healing and a much brighter future. Her story may provide just the inspiration a reader needs.

1. He was demoted at work.

2. She was fired from a job.

3. His partner cheated on him.

4. Her family member or best friend betrayed her.

5. He was bullied as a child.

6. She became the target of widespread online bullying.

7. He suffered a very dramatic public embarrassment.

8. Someone distributed nude photos or videos of her without her consent.

9. Her dog or cat died.

10. He survived cancer or another life-threatening physical illness.

11. She was scammed out of a bunch of money.

12. She was rejected from the college he'd always dreamed of attending.

13. He failed out of college or was unable to finish.

14. He didn't get the chance to go to college at all.

15. She got pregnant by accident.

16. She suffered a miscarriage.

17. They suffered as a result of infertility.

18. His new venture failed.

19. She was physically abused by parents, an older sibling, or someone else as a child.

20. They were emotionally abused as a child.

21. As an adult, he was physically or emotionally abused by his partner.

22. Her father physically abused her mother.

23. He was wrongfully accused of a crime.

24. She was arrested.

25. He went to prison.

26. Her mother or father went to prison.

27. When she was a child, her parents went through an ugly and protracted divorce.

28. His spouse divorced him and/or moved out with little warning.

29. Her fiancé called off the wedding.

30. Her ex-husband abandoned their children.

31. He lost access to his children.

32. She survived severe post-partum depression or a life-threatening mental illness.

33. His partner was severely mentally ill, exhausting him as a partner and caretaker.

34. Someone she loved had a serious illness or dementia, exhausting her as a caretaker.

35. His child had severe physical or behavioral issues, exhausting him as a parent.

36. Her child emotionally and/or physically abused her.

37. Her partner or someone she loved was an extreme addict.

38. Someone he loved committed a serious crime.

39. He or someone close to him was the victim of police brutality.

40. She or someone she loved was deported or forced into exile.

41. He was thrown out of his home or evicted without warning.

42. She lived in an unsafe place or a war zone.

43. They were the victim of a home invasion or forced to house soldiers.

44. His home was taken from him or destroyed.

45. She survived a hurricane, a tornado, a flood, a wildfire, or another disaster.

46. He lost his license or accreditation.

47. She was raised by parents who used her childhood as online content, forcing her to regularly perform for a huge number of followers.

48. He was rejected by his family or friends for his religious beliefs, political beliefs, sexual orientation, or another reason.

49. They were rejected at school or work for their race, their religion, or another aspect of their identity.

50. They survived a time of scarcity or famine.

51. She grew up in extreme poverty.

52. He grew up in a cult with psychologically damaging beliefs.

53. She suffered from memory loss or cognitive issues as the result of a stroke or a brain injury.

54. Someone poisoned her, or drugged her without her consent.

55. Without their consent, they were operated on or used as a subject in a medical experiment.

56. He survived a mass shooting, or a drive-by shooting in his home.

57. Someone she loved went missing.

58. One or both parents abandoned him when he was young.

59. One or both parents, or a sibling, died when he was young.

60. He was mauled by an aggressive dog or a wild animal.

61. She was mugged or robbed.

62. He was beaten up.

63. She was injured or disabled in an accident.

64. He sustained a career-ending injury or disability.

65. His spouse died.

66. One of her parents, a sibling, or a close friend died.

67. Their child died.

68. He fought in a war.

69. She witnessed a horrific accident or violent crime.

70. He witnessed the murder of someone he loved.

71. He was molested as a child.

72. She was sexually assaulted or raped as an adult.

73. Someone she loved commits suicide.

74. He accidentally killed a stranger or someone he loved.

75. She was tricked, brainwashed, or forced to kill a stranger or someone she loved.

50 WAYS TO SHOW A CHARACTER IS A GOOD PERSON

If a character's goodness or kindness is important to the story, then you'll probably want to show that in action. Sometimes, you want to establish right away that your character is a decent person at heart, even if they have flaws.

1. They say good morning to someone and ask about their weekend.

2. They smile at a stranger.

3. They listen to someone else's story—even if it's boring.

4. They really listen to a friend instead of just waiting for their turn to speak.

5. They sympathize with another person's gripes—even petty ones.

6. They treat an unpopular or odd person with respect.

7. They compliment something that somebody made.

8. They tell someone that their child, dog, or cat is adorable.

9. They tell someone that they are being too hard on themselves.

10. They give money to a panhandler when everyone else walks on by.

11. They know the name of their elderly neighbor or the security guard at their company.

12. They notice when someone appears to be lost or confused, and offer to help.

13. They call their mom or grandma.

14. They visit a sick friend or an aging relative.

15. They take care of a friend's or sibling's child for an afternoon or evening.

16. They dog-sit for someone who's on vacation.

17. They help catch a dog or cat who's gotten loose.

18. On their morning commute, they let someone merge in front of them.

19. When someone accidentally bumps into them, they say it's okay instead of getting annoyed.

20. When they have a legitimate customer complaint, they address it politely instead of rudely.

21. They confront someone who's bullying a sales associate, cashier, or server.

22. They donate blood.

23. They volunteer.

24. They hold the elevator door open for someone and say, "Take your time."

25. They give up their seat to someone else on the bus or train who needs it more.

26. At the grocery store, they let someone with just one or two items go ahead of them in line.

27. If someone is about to pay for something and realizes they're short a dollar or two, your character covers the difference.

28. They return their shopping cart to the corral.

29. They apologize when they've made a mistake.

30. After they shovel snow off their driveway, they shovel the neighbor's driveway, too.

31. They help someone whose car is stuck in the snow, or jumpstart their engine.

32. They write a nice comment on someone else's post or picture on social media.

33. They bring donuts—or homemade muffins—to the office.

34. They buy lemonade from the neighbor kids' lemonade stand.

35. They pretend to enjoy food someone has prepared, even though it's gross.

36. They decline to participate in gossip.

37. They're quick to give credit to a coworker.

39. They compliment someone in front of their family members or their peers.

40. When they're shopping for clothes, they pick up a shirt that slips off the hanger and return it to the rack.

41. They pray.

42. When they start speaking at the same time as someone else, they say, "Go ahead."

43. They find a recycling bin for their empty can or bottle.

44. They pick up a piece of trash and throw it away.

45. At a social event, they strike up a conversation with someone who's alone and looks ill at ease.

46. They compliment a child on their artwork or their outfit.

47. When they're running late in the morning, they turn back because they forgot to kiss their partner goodbye.

48. They call or text their partner in the middle of the day to say, "I love you."

49. They call their mom regularly.

50. They have an opportunity to steal or cheat with no chance of getting caught, but they don't do it.

50 WAYS TO SHOW A CHARACTER IS A JERK

Some of these things might give others the *impression* that your character is a jerk...when they're really not!

1. They give backhanded compliments.

2. They share a nasty rumor without being able to confirm it.

3. They're rude to the server or the person doing their nails.

4. They send back their order at a restaurant, even though it's really fine.

5. They don't throw away their trash at a fast food restaurant—they just leave it on the table.

8. They take up two spaces when they park their car.

9. They park in a spot reserved for the disabled, although they are able-bodied.

10. They honk their horn at other drivers, and even pedestrians, for minor infractions.

11. They demean their spouse, child, or friend in front of others, maybe in a joking way.

12. They make someone uncomfortable with their sexual talk or behavior.

13. They believe that insulting someone is a valid form of flirtation.

14. They don't say thank you.

15. They say "no" instead of "no thanks" to a polite request.

16. They write a vicious review of a student or community concert or play.

17. They borrow something without asking.

18. They insist upon being addressed more formally, such as "Doctor" or "Senator."

19. They make themselves too comfortable in a space that isn't their own: putting their feet on someone else's desk, for example.

20. They give unsolicited and bossy advice.

21. They ask someone about their private business when many others are around to hear.

22. They decline to sponsor a walkathon or order Girl Scout cookies.

23. They complain about crying babies or loud little kids.

24. If they don't get someone's attention immediately, they are rude about it: they say, "Hellooo…" or snap their fingers at them.

25. They let people know exactly what kinds of gifts they will find acceptable.

26. They issue detailed and demanding instructions to the wedding party or to everyone coming over for Thanksgiving.

27. They get angry with their parents or grandparents for not providing child care on a regular basis, or for spending money on travel instead of saving it so the next generation can inherit it.

28. They make fun of people who aren't hurting anyone, either behind their backs or to their faces.

29. They make negative generalizations about large groups of people.

30. If someone calls them on the mean thing they said, that person is just "too sensitive" because "it was just a joke."

31. They fake-lunge at someone to make them flinch, as a joke.

32. They look up to or suck up to a wealthy or powerful person, even if that person is a bully.

33. They let others know that their new designer handbag or their car was very expensive.

34. They take a friendly game way too seriously. They *have* to win.

35. They always walk too fast, even though their significant other has told them many times that they're struggling to keep up.

36. They always turn the subject of a conversation back to themselves.

37. They never pass up the opportunity to show how smart or successful they are.

38. They are the expert, no matter what the topic is.

39. They blame people for their own hardships. That college graduate should've majored in another field if they wanted to find a job; that sick relative wouldn't have gotten sick if they'd lost some weight.

40. They tell someone who's sad or disappointed that "it's not that big of a deal" and "they're being overdramatic."

41. They're never genuinely happy for another person's happiness, success, or good luck.

42. When another person does something good, they ascribe selfish motives to it; the person just wanted attention, for instance.

43. They look down on people's hobbies or other harmless things that bring them joy.

44. They get annoyed with someone for struggling to speak and understand English, or for having trouble hearing a conversation.

45. You feel like you have to be on your guard when you're around them.

46. Although their negativity is subtle, you often feel drained after spending time with them.

47. According to them, all of their exes are crazy, and all of their coworkers are awful.

48. Their friends are jerks.

49. They refuse to admit they were wrong. It wasn't technically wrong, it was someone else's fault, or it was no big deal.

50. Your dog or your grandma doesn't like them—and your dog or your grandma likes everybody.

50 CHARACTER ARCS

A character arc is the way a character learns, grows, or changes over the course of a story. In other words, the character we see at the end of the book isn't the same person we met on page one.

While character arcs in books and movies are often positive, remember that it's also possible for someone to have a negative character arc or to become worse. Sometimes this is referred to as a *character corruption arc* or a villain origin story. I've included a few examples of this, and of course, any of the heroic character arcs here can be reversed.

Book editors and producers like to see clear character arcs, and understanding them can make writing—and revising—a novel, story, or screenplay a whole lot easier.

1. They overcome their guilt over a tragedy and return to work or to battle…or let themselves love again.

2. They recognize their past wrongs and attempt to apologize and/or make amends.

3. They let down their guard so they can be close to a person, or to a group of people.

4. They finally give up on an unrequited love and turn their attention to something that will make them happier.

5. They learn that they have a lot to be grateful for in their life, just as it is.

6. They start prioritizing their relationships over their career.

7. They become more disciplined and hard-working.

8. They gain or regain confidence.

9. They gain or regain spiritual faith.

10. They learn the truth about their family, company, community, or government and become disenchanted.

11. They learn to work with others instead of always being in charge.

12. They step up as a leader for the first time.

13. They let go of a long-held resentment or grudge.

14. They become more willing to lie, steal, or even kill in the service of what they believe is a greater moral cause.

15. They become highly skilled in battle.

16. They go from putting a cause first to putting the welfare of a certain person first.

17. They kick a habit or addiction.

18. They assimilate to a new lifestyle or society.

19. They become a congenial person who enjoys the company of others.

20. They overcome their pessimism and start looking on the bright side.

21. They embrace their innate identity.

22. They learn to trust their gut instincts instead of overthinking everything.

23. They leave behind a life of crime.

24. Once set in their ways, they become willing to try new things.

25. Once a warrior, they become a pacifist or someone who strives for peace.

26. They stop associating their worth with their family or their title.

27. They start being honest about their lives instead of maintaining a perfect facade.

28. They overcome their pride and ask for help.

29. They start paying attention to their own needs and desires, and not just their family's.

30. They break a taboo or flout a societal norm in order to pursue their bliss.

31. They give up on making elaborate plans and go with the flow.

32. They go from faking an interest in something to actually feeling it.

33. They learn that they can't trust everyone.

34. They stop trying to manage their children's or their friends' lives.

35. They become tougher or more resilient.

36. They learn to not take on more than they can handle.

37. They're no longer willing to take big risks with their life because they have something to live for.

38. They go from being the prey to being the hunter.

39. They become loyal to someone they originally distrusted or despised.

40. They become more independent—financially, and/or in terms of decision-making.

41. After years of dating many people, none of them seriously, they decide to make a go of a serious romantic relationship.

42. They overcome a bias or prejudice.

43. They give up on civility and become rough and brutal.

44. They become a public figure who is very calculated about messages and appearances.

45. Once an honest person, they gradually become someone who will lie and cheat to hold onto money or power—or gain even more of it.

45. In a conflict or a battle, they begin acting strategically rather than rashly.

46. They go from not being a fan of dogs, cats, or children to liking them.

47. They stop blaming other people and bad luck for all their problems and start taking accountability for their own actions.

48. They let go of an old career or business dream in order to pursue a new one.

49. Once stingy, they become willing to spend money on loved ones, on their own enjoyment, and/or on good causes.

50. They stop endlessly striving to be perfect and start accepting themselves for who they are.

TITLES

Many writers agonize over the title of their book, short story, or screenplay, and with good reason. A great title makes a strong positive impression on an agent, an editor, a reader, or a moviegoer.

In most cases, a successful title doesn't sound like it belongs to a different genre. For instance, if you've written a romance novel, you probably don't want it to sound like a nonfiction book about personal finance.

It's usually a good idea to aim for a title that's easy for people to remember and recommend. That can often mean keeping the title short. Another benefit of keeping a title short—and keeping the *words* in the title short—is that the title can be larger on the cover, which can make it stand out to potential readers. But with writing, there are never any hard and fast rules, and some books with long titles become bestsellers.

I hope the so-called formulas in this section help you as you brainstorm the perfect title!

15 GREAT FORMULAS FOR TITLES

1. Use an "open loop."

"Open loop" is an old-school term in advertising copywriting. It means leaving out some key information—in other words, not closing the loop—in order to pique the reader's curiosity. You've seen this approach in entertainment news ("Actor Reveals the Heartbreaking Reason He Left the Show") and in online advertising ("Get Better Sleep With This One Weird Trick!")

Examples:

> *It Ends With Us*, Colleen Hoover
>
> *Can You Forgive Her?*, Anthony Trollope
>
> *I Know Why the Caged Bird Sings*, Maya Angelou
>
> *The Most Fun We Ever Had*, Claire Lombardo
>
> *The Perks of Being a Wallflower*, Stephen Chbosky
>
> *Things We Left Behind*, Lucy Score

2. Use this construction: *adjective noun.*

This is one of the most common approaches to a book title.

Examples:

> *Wolf Hall*, Hilary Mantel
>
> *The Hunger Games*, Suzanne Collins
>
> *The Round House*, Louise Erdrich
>
> *The Great Gatsby*, F. Scott Fitzgerald
>
> *The Secret History*, Donna Tartt
>
> *Lonesome Dove*, Larry McMurtry

3. Use this construction: *noun* and *noun.*

Examples:

>*War and Peace*, Leo Tolstoy
>
>*The Master And Margarita*, Mikhail Bulgakov
>
>*Cat & Mouse*, James Patterson
>
>*Pride and Prejudice*, Jane Austen
>
>*Fates and Furies*, Lauren Groff

4. Use a character's name.

Examples:

>*Don Quixote*, Miguel de Cervantes
>
>*Bridget Jones's Diary*, Helen Fielding
>
>*Rebecca*, Daphne DuMaurier
>
>*Giovanni's Room*, James Baldwin
>
>*The Song of Achilles*, Madeline Miller
>
>*Frankenstein*, Mary Shelley

5. Use the character's job or role, real or symbolic, in the story.

Examples:

>*The Invisible Man*, Ralph Ellison
>
>*Interpreter of Maladies*, J. Lahiri
>
>*The Housemaid*, Freida McFadden
>
>*Vampires of El Norte*, Isabel Cañas

6. Include a number.

Examples:

>*The Three Musketeers,* Alexandre Dumas
>
>*The Seven Husbands of Evelyn Hugo*, Taylor Jenkins Reid
>
>*Twenty Thousand Leagues Under the Sea*, Jules Verne

The Four Winds, Kristin Hannah

Slaughterhouse-Five, Kurt Vonnegut, Jr.

7. Use a title that's a command.

Examples:

Dance Upon the Air, Nora Roberts

Never Let Me Go, Kazuo Ishiguro

Call Me By Your Name, André Aciman

Play It As It Lays, Joan Didion

Meet Me at the Lake, Carley Fortune

8. Include a month or a season.

Examples:

Across Five Aprils, Irene Hunt

Devil in Winter, Lisa Kleypas

The Summer I Turned Pretty, Jenny Han

The Hunt for Red October, Tom Clancy

9. Use a city, state, country, or other geographical feature.

Examples:

Harlem Shuffle, Colson Whitehead

A Gentleman in Moscow, Amor Towles

Washington Square, Henry James

The Paris Library, Janet Skeslien Charles

The Guernsey Literary and Potato Peel Pie Society, Mary Ann Shaffer, Annie Barrows

10. Use a phrase from the Bible, Shakespeare, or another work in the public domain.

"In the public domain" means that the work is no longer protected by copyright, usually because it's so old that the copyright has expired. Keep in mind, though, that English language translations of old works in other languages may still be copyrighted.

Examples:

> *Stranger in a Strange Land*, Robert A. Heinlein (from Exodus 2:22, the Bible)
>
> *The Fault in Our Stars*, John Green (adapted from *Julius Caesar*, Shakespeare)
>
> *Things Fall Apart*, Chinua Achebe (from "The Second Coming," W.B. Yeats)
>
> *All the King's Men*, Robert Penn Warren (from the nursery rhyme "Humpty Dumpty")
>
> *Tomorrow and Tomorrow and Tomorrow*, Gabrielle Zevin (*Macbeth*, Shakespeare)

11. Steal a song title.

Song titles aren't protected by copyright, which is why books sometimes use them.

Examples:

> *Devil In a Blue Dress*, Walter Mosley
>
> *Norwegian Wood*, Haruki Murakami
>
> *All the Pretty Horses*, Cormac McCarthy (after the lullaby "All the Pretty Little Horses")
>
> *This Must Be the Place*, Maggie O'Farrell
>
> *All Things Bright and Beautiful*, James Herriot

12. Use a familiar phrase—or put a spin on it.

Examples:

The Best Laid Plans, Sidney Sheldon

You Only Live Twice, Ian Fleming

The Heart of the Matter, Graham Greene

Dearly Beloved, Anne Morrow Lindbergh

13. Use a play on words. This approach is especially popular in romance and cozy mystery.

Examples:

Equal Rites, Terry Pratchett

Who's Afraid of Virginia Woolf?, Edward Albee

The Hating Game, Sally Thorne

Under Loch and Key, Lana Ferguson

The Quiche of Death, M.C. Beaton

14. Use just one word with a dramatic impact.

Examples:

Disgrace, JM Coetzee

Jaws, Peter Benchley

Dune, Frank Herbert

Eragon, Christopher Paolini

Roots, Alex Haley

It, Stephen King

15. Use one or more words that are aligned with the genre.

For instance, if you're writing a murder mystery, your title could include a word like *murder, kill,* or *death,* and if you're writing a time travel story, you might put the word *time* in the title.

Examples:

> *A Game of Thrones*, George R.R. Martin
>
> *The Kiss Quotient*, Helen Hoang
>
> *How to Sell a Haunted House*, Grady Hendrix
>
> *The Thursday Murder Club*, Richard Osman
>
> *Tinker, Tailor, Soldier, Spy*, John Le Carré
>
> *Her Time Traveling Duke*, Bryn Donovan

On the following pages, I have lists of "genre words" for mystery/ thriller, romance, and fantasy that might inspire you to come up with this kind of title. Many of these aren't as obvious as the examples above, but they're appropriate. Some of these words are very expected, but you can combine them with words that are less expected—or just use them to spark your imagination as you think about your title.

GENRE WORDS: MYSTERY/THRILLER

Many words on this list would work for horror, too. Naturally, there's also considerable overlap with the fantasy list, since that genre frequently features life-and-death stakes.

accused	captive	deceit
agent	case	deception
alias	cause	degree
alibi	cell	deep
arrest	classified	departed
ashes	clue	defense
assassin	code	depths
backlash	cold	desperate
below	confidential	destroy
beneath	conspiracy	devil
betrayal	control	die
beware	crime	disappear
blade	criminal	dossier
blood	cruel	doubt
body	cut	duty
bones	damage	edge
break	danger	end
brief	dangerous	enemy
broken	dare	escape
brutal	dark	evidence
burn	dead	evil
bury	deadly	execution
buried	death	exit

extreme	judge	payback
factor	jury	past
fail	justice	plan
false	kill	plot
fatal	killer	poison
fear	killing	power
file(s)	key	private
final	knife	prey
fire	last	proof
follow	law	protocol
force	lawyer	quiet
foul	lethal	rage
fugitive	lies	remains
funeral	lost	requiem
gone	malice	revenge
grave	mayhem	risk
ground	mercy	rival
grounds	midnight	rogue
guilt	missing	ruin
guilty	mission	run
hard	money	savage
harm	mortal	secrets
hidden	motive	sentence
honor	murder	shadow
hunt	mystery	shot
hush	night	silent
innocence	notorious	sin
innocent	nowhere	skeleton
intent	offense	skull

search	threat	violent
sentence	tomb	violence
sleep	traitor	wanted
spy	treachery	warning
state	trouble	watch
steal	true	weapon
stolen	truth	wicked
storm	twisted	will
stranger	unknown	witness
survivor	vanish	wrong
suspect	vendetta	wrongful
target	vengeance	zero
terminal	verdict	
testament	vice	
testimony	victim	
thief	vile	

GENRE WORDS: ROMANCE

Romantic suspense authors might also find inspiration in the previous list of words for mysteries and thrillers, and romantasy authors might want to check out the list of fantasy words. A few of these words may sound negative for romance, but keep in mind that romance authors often work in tropes like enemies to lovers and forbidden romance, and romcom authors sometimes use negative words for comic effect.

adore	breath	dare
affair	bride	dark
all	bridesmaid	date
always	burn	deep
arrange	captivate	devoted
arrangement	catch	devotion
attract	chance	desire
attraction	charm	destiny
baby	chase	dream
bad	cherish	embrace
beautiful	choose	enchant
belong	claim	engagement
best	come	entice
best man	connection	entrance
bewitch	couple	eternal
blooms	courtship	eternity
boss	crave	ex
boy	crush	faithful
boyfriend	cute	fake
breakup	dance	fall(ing)

fate	him	mistake
favorite	his	moon
feeling(s)	home	moonlight
fever	honeymoon	my
fiancé	honor	mine
fiancée	hope	need
fierce	hot	night
find	husband	obsession
first	irresistible	once
flames	joy	one
forbidden	keep	only
flirt	kiss	our
forever	letters	pact
friend	life	pair
game	lifetime	paradise
gift(s)	like	passion
girl	last	perfect
girlfriend	love	perfection
give	lovely	persuade
good	lover	pleasure
groom	lost	possess
guy	lucky	promise
hand(s)	marriage	rain
have	marry	ravish
hate	match	ready
heart	mate	reckless
heat	meet	remember
heaven	memory	rescue
her(s)	midnight	return

reunited	sunshine	tryst
right	spice	twisted
romance	stars	two
roommate	steal	undone
rose(s)	storm	us
rescue	sunset	valentine
ruin	surrender	veil
rule	sweet	vow
safe	swept	want
save	take	we
savor	taste	wedding
say	tell	whisper
scandal	tempt	wicked
second chance	temptation	wife
secret	time	wild
seduce	together	wish
share	touch	words
sin/sinful	treasure(s)	worse
single	true	worst
someone	truly	you
song	trust	your(s)

GENRE WORDS: FANTASY

ancient	children	dusk
age	choice	duty
angel	chosen	earth
arcane	chronicle	elf
arcana	city	emperor
army	council	empire
arrow	court	empress
ash	crow	enchant
assassin	crown	enchantment
axe	crystal	enemy
battle	curse	exile
beast	dark	fae
blade	darkness	fairy
black	daughter	fall
blood	dawn	fallen
bone	day	fate
book	dead	fire
bound	decree	forge
breath	demon	forest
broken	destiny	fortress
call	divine	frost
castle	djinn	fury
cave	door	garden
chains	dragon	gate
chaos	dream	gift
child	druid	god

goddess	league	prisoner
gold	legacy	prophecy
guardian	legend	queen
hand	light	quest
harp	liar	rage
hawk	lion	raven
healer	lord	realm
helm	lost	rebel
heir	mage	red
hero	magic	relic
honor	magician	rider
house	majesty	ring
ice	map	rival
immortal	mirror	river
infinite	mist	rise
infinity	monster	rising
iron	moon	ruin
ivory	mountain	rule
isle	myth	rune
jewel	name	saint
justice	oath	scroll
keep	obsidian	sea
keeper	omen	secret
key	order	seer
king	paladin	serpent
kingdom	poison	servant
knight	power	shadow
lady	prince	shield
land	princess	ship

silver	thief	wayfarer
siren	thorn	weave
sky	thread	weaver
smoke	time	white
snow	tide	wing
son	throne	winter
sorcerer	tower	witch
sorceress	traitor	wind
soul	tree	wizard
spear	unbound	wolf
spell	veil	wraith
steel	vine	wrath
stolen	vow	
stone	voyage	
storm	wall	
sun	war	
sword	warrior	
tale	water	
temple	way	

10 REASONS WHY YOU SHOULD WRITE THAT STORY

1. Because nobody else can write it but you.

Your beliefs, your knowledge, your brain chemistry, plus the sum total of all your experiences, make you absolutely unique in the world. Nobody can write the exact story you can. If you don't write it, it will never exist.

2. Because you're not alone.

If you're into it, someone else out there will be, too. Even if you believe your story is niche or unusual, other people share some of your interests or experiences. The audience may be small, or it may be huge. Either way, it exists. If your story is different, the people who love that kind of story will be all the more grateful to find it.

3. Because your life will go by either way.

Some people worry about how much time it will take them to finish a project. What if it takes a whole year? What if it takes three? Three years from now, you will be three years older, and you can do that with or without a finished story (or two, or ten.) Your choice.

4. Because you're not too young.

If you're young, it's the perfect time to learn. If you work hard and seek out opportunities to learn, you can start becoming proficient at your craft right now.

5. Because you're not too old.

Writing isn't like being an Olympic figure skater. As long as your mind is still working, you can write a story. As you get older, you know more about life and have had more experiences, and that will only make your writing better.

6. Because you have the right.

Some people tell themselves that they aren't smart enough or creative enough to attempt writing—even when they want to. They wonder if they can tell extraordinary stories when their lives are so ordinary. Others worry that people will judge them for writing ("Who do you think you are?"), or judge them for writing in a certain genre ("Comic books, really?") You have as much right as anybody else to tell stories, plus the right to ignore anyone who says otherwise.

7. Because it doesn't have to be perfect.

Perfectionism can keep people from daring to write their story—or to finish it. If it's your very first story, it doesn't ever have to be good. Nobody paints a museum-worthy masterpiece the first time they pick up a brush. Learning and struggling aren't shameful, but reasons to feel proud.

Some of the greatest stories have flaws that everyone acknowledges. Good writing isn't just about getting rid of flaws, but also about building on your strengths—and entertaining, enlightening, and inspiring.

Besides, no matter how proficient you get, no story ever has to be good in the rough draft stage. It's the final draft that counts.

8. Because you'll never know how good it can be until you try.

It might be brilliant.

9. Because you have complete control over it.

If you're like most people, you don't get to control everything in your life. The behavior of the people around you, the stock market, the weather—for better or worse, you have to just deal with these things. In your story, you are in charge. Like an all-powerful deity, you can create an entire world, and the people who populate it. If you get an offer with a publishing company, you may agree to changes in the story, but that's your decision.

10. Because if you don't, you might wish you had later.

You don't ever want to look back with regrets. So write it, and have fun!